LOUIS

ACKNOWLEDGEMENTS

With a mind that rarely settles on any one thing for very long, it was never going to be easy for me to write this book. Luckily, I had a lot of help from some special people who I would like to thank here.

Firstly, my mum, Elaine who can remember every move I made as a kid (and there were a lot of them). She's always supported me in everything I've done and has sacrificed so much of her own life over the years to help me devote myself to doing gym. She's my angel and I wouldn't have achieved anything like what I have done without her love and support. The same goes for my older brother, Leon and of course my nan, Dilys, who sadly wasn't able to see me compete at London 2012, but who I know is always looking over me from up on high.

My coach, Paul Hall, is another person to whom I owe so much for his guidance, friendship and endless support. Ever since he first invited me into his training group when I was a cheeky seven year old, he has been someone I could always turn to and is simply one of the best gymnastics coaches out there.

My agent, Gab Stone, has become a hugely important person in my life since we met in Beijing five years ago, both in a business and a personal sense. This book was his idea, too, so this is probably the right place to admit that occasionally, he does come up with some very good ideas (not that I'd ever tell him that).

A big thank you also goes to Jane Sturrock and Nicola Crossley at Orion Books for their enthusiasm and help with my book, to Sarah Shephard for helping me to tell my story (as well as to *Sport* magazine for lending her to me) and to everyone at GSE Management.

To all my GB gymnastics teammates and my *Strictly* family – you have all played a huge role in helping to make my story one worth telling, so thank you.

And of course, to all my friends – those mentioned in the book and the rest of you – thank you for being my escape from gym when I've needed it and for always treating me like the Lou you've always known.

CONTENTS

2012: FOUR LITTLE NUMBERS WHICH, WHEN LINED UP SIDE BY SIDE, ADD UP TO THE GREATEST YEAR OF MY LIFE – MY LIFE SO FAR, THAT IS.

I was still living at home with my mum when the announcement was made that London would host the 2012 Olympic Games. I didn't have any responsibilities like bills to pay or exams to study for so that event became like a goal for me – something to work towards and pull me through every gruelling session in the gym. From that amazing July day onwards, London 2012 was my final target to try and reach.

Everything I did was with London 2012 in mind. Even when I was competing in the Beijing Olympics, I really felt it was more of a stepping stone to something altogether bigger and better to come in four years' time. When you have such a massive goal in front of you, it's difficult to see anything beyond it, so I never really gave too much thought to what might happen once the Games were over.

Well, this book is part of that. It's a chance for me to look back at a journey that so far has taken me from being a troublesome kid whose appetite for mischief knew no bounds, to an adult with three Olympic medals, an MBE from the Queen and a glitterball trophy for ballroom dancing.

If you'd have told me any of that was possible back in the days when I was more into break dancing than ballroom and my gymnastics coach was driven to despair by my antics on a daily basis, I would have called you crazy.

As it turned out, 2012 itself was crazy. It was the end of a long, hard but ultimately amazing chapter for me – one which I have loved re-living over the following pages. This is my story so far, I hope you enjoy it as much as I have.

Lewis

1

Born to perform

If you've ever tried supporting all your bodyweight on just your arms, and holding it for around 50 seconds, then you'll know a little bit about the pain. It starts in your wrists, moves up into your forearms and gradually spreads through all the muscles in your upper arms and into your shoulders, where it starts screaming at you to stop. That is the pain of the pommel horse in gymnastics, and it's one I've become intimately familiar with throughout my career.

The screaming never goes away, it's always there, in the last few seconds of every routine and the last few routines of every training session. But you learn to ignore it – to block out the pain and the noise until that blissful moment when your feet touch the floor after a successful dismount.

To everyone watching, it looks easy. It looks effortless. It looks like two Olympic Games and three Olympic medals came my way without dropping so much as a bead of sweat. And most of all, it looks as though I did it all on my own. None of which – especially the latter – are remotely true.

If you took the person I am now and hit the rewind button back to when I was a kid, you would see me get a lot smaller (obviously), my hair get much bigger, and you'd watch a pretty chilled, mature adult turn into a hyperactive, nightmare child without an off switch.

I cringe now at some of the things I put Mum through. Elaine, as she's known to everyone except my brother Leon and me, raised us mostly on her own, after my dad, Claude, left when I was three years old. I call her my guardian angel and it's no exaggeration to say that I wouldn't have achieved anywhere near as much as I have without without her help and constant support.

From the minute we were born and while we were growing up, Mum made sure that Leon and I had the best of everything she could afford. She worked part-time as a hairdresser, fitting her hours in around looking after us, but money was always really tight and she had to go without a lot of things so that we could have a new computer game or a pair of trainers.

My nan, Dilys, made life a bit easier for her. Mum never had to pay for a babysitter to look after us because Nan was always there; she was like a second mum to us. She was Welsh and a little bit crazy, but lovely. When I was really young I'd spend loads of time at her house, which was about 15 minutes away from Mum's, playing Mousetrap and messing around on my bike or the little skateboard I used to have.

From the minute we were born and while we were growing up, Mum made sure that Leon and I had the best of everything she could afford.

It was Nan who first taught me how to ride a bike, not that I needed much teaching, but she was there watching in case I fell off. She helped me to learn my numbers and taught me to whistle and catch a ball, too. She was a constant presence in our lives. Whenever me or Leon were in school plays, Nan would come to watch, and when I started competing in gymnastics she was always there, too. Even when she got older and

couldn't travel so much, she'd come to the gym instead. They would find her a little chair to sit on and she'd stay there for hours, watching me train. Whenever I came back from a competition, the first thing I would do is go straight to see Nan to show her my medal – she loved everything about me doing gym.

Neither me or Leon ever got to meet our grandad as he sadly passed away when Mum was pregnant with Leon, so it was really just the three of us during those early years. I would speak to my dad, Claude, on the phone now and again – as I still do – but we only saw him once or twice a year. I have a good relationship with my dad now, but I wouldn't say he plays an active role in my life. Mum has never dated anyone else, either; she always said she had more than enough on her plate with looking after two young boys, and that she wouldn't want anyone to get in the way of that.

Leon used to feel like it was his role to look after me, too. He's three and a half years older than me and has always been a really protective big brother. He'd watch over me all the time when we were younger,

and would always let everyone know that if they upset his little bro' they would have him to deal with.

He threw himself into action once, when I was about three years old and he came with Mum and Nan to pick me up from the play centre. As they arrived they saw me waiting outside with another little boy who was grabbing me by the wrist and swinging me round so fast my legs would come off the floor. What they didn't realise was that we were just playing. All Leon saw was this boy holding me by the wrists, so he ran over and launched himself at the other boy, drop-kicking him in the chest before Mum or Nan had a chance to stop him.

Our relationship is probably even better now than it was when we were younger. We live near to each other and see each other whenever we can, usually at Mum's so she can cook us dinner. He isn't a huge fan of being in the public eye and tends to stay away from events where he knows there will be a lot of press, so it meant a lot when he came to watch me compete at London 2012.

So many people have tried to interview him about me. One of the *Strictly Come Dancing* producers met him at the Olympic Games and thought he was really funny, so she was desperate for him to be part of the little video interviews they did with Mum during the series, but he wasn't having any of it. He watched every single show on TV though, and would ring me after every one. When we see each other these days he likes to just do normal stuff – play PlayStation or go for a quiet drink – anything that doesn't involve cameras, journalists or newspapers. He'll still jump to my defence if he thinks someone's doing wrong by me. He'll still be doing that even when we're a pair of wrinkly old pensioners.

When I was a kid, it was like I was on a constant energy buzz; I was always climbing up things, jumping over stuff and running around like a crazy puppy that's just been let off a leash. So it's little wonder that I managed to break two bones in the space of six months. The first time it was my wrist. I told Mum that it had happened when Leon had pushed me off the fence, but I can't even remember if that was true or not.

The second time I think we'd been climbing in the garden and I ran into the house and said, 'Mum, I've broken my arm.' She said, 'No you haven't Louis,' thinking I was just being dramatic after what had happened last time. I told her I had and that I'd heard it crack. So it was back to hospital for us both, where I ended up having some metal pins put into my arm.

The doctor was quite impressed, in a way. He said I was obviously landing with my arms out to protect myself, which showed good instincts. And when he saw my legs, which were covered in bruises from the shin down, he said I was clearly a very active child. His suggestion was that Mum should get me involved in something that would help me to burn off some energy a bit more safely.

That would come soon, but first it was off to nursery, where I was still running around like a crazed animal. The teachers there told Mum that if they made me sit down and do a puzzle, I'd actually be sweating with

the effort of just sitting and concentrating. They compared me to a little dog desperate to be let out for a run.

In my first year at school, too, I used to do the teachers' heads in. One of them once told Mum that I was a loveable little boy, but that because I couldn't concentrate on anything I was constantly on the move, like a headless chicken. In those days, Mum just put it down to being overactive, so she started to find lots of activities for me to do after school – anything that might tire me out a bit.

Me and Leon would both go to the local sports centre where we could play all sorts of sports and it was Leon who was brilliant at all of them. Anything he put his mind to, he would be good at – football, boxing, basketball, anything – but he never pursued any of them. Once he got bored with something, that would be it, he'd stop. He would never push through that barrier and keep going. That's where we're quite different, because I like to try and be the best at anything I do, and I'll keep going until I'm sure I've given it everything I've got.

When I was four, Mum started taking Leon to a gymnastics group near where we lived in Werrington, and she would take me along too. I would sit and watch what the boys there were doing, itching to join in, but they only coached boys from the age of six, so Mum said I would have to wait a couple of years before I could start.

At home, I started to copy what I'd seen my brother and the others doing at the gym and Mum realised it was something I would really enjoy. She also thought it might be something that would finally use up enough of my excess energy to make me less of a problem child. She explained what I'd been doing at home to the head coach at Werrington and asked if they could make an exception and take me on, even though I was only four.

That was the start of everything. Gymnastics was a sport I took to straight away and I was doing things at the age of four that the boys of my brother's age were doing. I loved it too, which meant that I actually wanted to learn, and the more I learnt, the more interesting it became.

I enjoyed playing other sports, like football, but to me it was always the same thing, running up and down the pitch for ages, chasing a ball. In the gym there was always something different to do.

It wasn't long before the teachers at Werrington noticed how quickly I picked up new skills in the gym and told Mum that I had the potential to be quite good. But they said that if she really wanted me to progress, she should take me to a gym in Huntingdon, which was about 26 miles away from where we lived. They said it was 'the best you're going to get' in terms of gymnastics training, so Mum decided we should at least go and see if they would take me on.

I had to do a mini trial at Huntingdon, so they could have a look at how my body moved, how flexible I was and see what I had already learned, and they were happy enough to sign me up. A 52-mile round trip was a long way for Mum to drive though, so to start with she would take me to Huntingdon two nights a week and I would still go to Werrington on another two or three nights: she liked me to do some sort of after-school activity every night if possible.

By the age of seven, I was training at Huntingdon every weeknight as well as on Sunday afternoons. Nan had to help Mum out with the petrol cost – a 52-mile round trip almost every day of the week was costing her a fortune, on top of paying gym fees and making sure I had enough kit. On weekdays, Mum would pick me up from school with a packed dinner in the car and a change of clothes. I'd eat on the way to Huntingdon and then Mum would have to wait for a few hours while I trained, before driving us home again. They were late nights and long days, and Mum would live like that for the next eleven years, but she knew it was doing me good, so she sacrificed all her own time to take me. There was nothing really stopping her from saying, 'I'm going to be a full-time hairdresser and make some decent money, sod the gym,' but she just kept on driving me back and forth to training.

Even though the gym was giving me some focus, I was still struggling to concentrate in school and a lot of the time – even in the gym – I would

run around like I'd swallowed ten packs of sugar or something. It was while she was there, watching me train one day, that Mum got talking to an American woman about how active I was. She explained that she was running out of ideas on how to tire me out and how badly I was sleeping at night.

The woman asked Mum if she had ever heard of ADHD, or Attention Deficit Hyperactivity Disorder, because she thought it sounded like I might have it. At that time, ADHD wasn't very well known or talked about in the UK, and Mum didn't know what it was, so as soon as she got home from the gym, she looked it up on the Internet.

As soon as she read the description of the symptoms ('those affected have a greatly reduced ability to maintain attention without being distracted . . . and to control the amount of physical activity appropriate to the situation – that is, they're restless and fidgety'), Mum was like, 'Oh my God, that's Louis.' She printed it off and brought it with her when she came to pick me up from school the next day.

Mum showed it to my teacher and asked her to read it, to see if it sounded like me. My teacher agreed with her entirely, saying it was a really accurate description of what I was like. But she didn't really know what that meant for me or what the next step should be.

Mum decided to ring one of her friends who is a social worker; she advised Mum to tell the doctor that she wanted me to be referred to a specialist consultant for ADHD. I remember when we first went to see the specialist. Well, I remember that she was a black lady and had a very soothing voice, so I know what she looked like but I don't know what they used to talk about.

Obviously, they were talking about me, but I would never listen. I just remember playing with the toys that were in her office. She had those domino bricks that you line up and then when you knock one down, it sets the whole lot off. I would build massive lines of them, winding through the legs of all the chairs around the room. Then, at the end of their meeting, they would measure and weigh me and we'd go home.

After a few of these visits to the specialist, she officially diagnosed me as having ADHD and talked Mum through all the different medicines I could take that might help me. The one she recommended was called Ritalin, which they started me on at the age of seven. I was kept on quite a high dose of it until I was 11, but even then we still had to see the specialist every three months to talk about how I was getting on at school and in the gym.

All I remember about taking the Ritalin is that it wasn't a nice tablet. It made me feel a bit like a zombie. It was weird because I knew that I still *wanted* to mess around but I just couldn't be bothered to. I can't tell you how frustrating that was. It was like two different parts of my brain wanted two completely different things, and the part that wanted me to sit down and shut up would always win.

The Ritalin did make a difference to my ability to concentrate, though. Not long after I went on it, one of the coaches at the gym told Mum they'd had a year's worth of work out of me in just a few hours, because I was so much more focused.

Mum kept me on Ritalin throughout junior school, but decided I needed a break from it before I started secondary school. When the new term was about to begin, I told her I didn't want to go back on it and that it made me feel sick. Being off it over the holidays had made me realise how much Ritalin was changing me, and I didn't want to go back to being that other person; it would have felt like putting a straitjacket on. Mum was worried about how I would cope with the double whammy of starting a new school and being off Ritalin, but agreed that we could at least try it.

After that, there was a brief spell when Mum made me go back on Ritalin for a bit – probably after a day when I'd been up to all sorts of mischief at school – and it was shit. I think I only took it for about two weeks and it made me feel awful. I'd sit in my classroom at lunchtime and just want to sleep – that's not normal for a 13-year-old lad. It wasn't nice at all.

When I came off Ritalin, I did find it a bit harder to focus but then, that's me. That's who I am. I didn't feel that taking it was right for me – anything that makes you feel 'zombified' surely can't be good for you. I can understand now that I'm older why they put me on it, because I was a little shit and Mum was on her own trying to cope with the child from hell, who had more energy than he knew what to do with. It makes sense that they'd try whatever they could to calm me down, but I'm still not sure I'd put my own child on it, knowing how it had made me feel.

Being at the gym was always easier for me than being at school. In a classroom, the teachers set you work and you either get on with it or you sit there getting bored, and most of the time I'd do the latter. But in the gym, I was constantly being given new things to do; I never got the chance to be bored. My coach always said that he never really noticed the difference between when I was on Ritalin and when I wasn't – either way I was the same active boy who couldn't concentrate on one thing longer than five minutes.

Over time though, gymnastics is a sport that teaches you structure and discipline, which is why the ADHD specialist told Mum it was such a good activity for me. Gymnastics was originally based on military exercises by the ancient Greeks and I think that discipline is still a massive part of gymnastics. It taught me to be on time, to be respectful and to work hard – all general life skills. I suppose you could almost say that gymnastics has been like another parent to me; it's certainly helped to make me who I am today.

Being at the gym was always easier for me than being at school.

You walk into training, stand in a line and shake your coach by the hand before every session. And in competition, when you finish your routine, you stand there and wait for the judges to make their decision. And you won't often see gymnasts showing their emotions when they land a routine. Even if you've really messed it up, you wait until you leave the apparatus area before letting it all out. There are exceptions, like when I couldn't hold back the tears after qualifying at London 2012, but most of the time gymnasts are so disciplined that they could fall off their apparatus twice, do a 'face plant' into the crash mat, get back on and still finish off their routine, raise an arm and force a big smile for the judges.

It's all part of the performance, I suppose, and performing is something I have been doing ever since I was tiny. Mum loves telling people how outgoing I was as a kid, even though she used to spend half the time hiding behind her hands when I was dancing, singing or just doing whatever I could to entertain people.

It didn't matter where I was, I would put on a show. I was at the doctors with Mum and Leon when I was about two and a half and they normally played bland, boring music in the waiting room, the kind of music you can just ignore. But a Michael Jackson song came on while we were there, and when I was a kid he was my idol. I loved watching him dance. So I started dancing in the doctor's surgery – moonwalking and thrusting my hips around the waiting room, in front of all the old people sitting waiting to go in. When the song finished they started clapping me, so I shouted, 'Do you want me to do it again?'

I just wasn't bothered by people looking at me – it was something I enjoyed. Mum's friend took me to the circus once with her two sons, and the clown came over to us during the show to ask if one of the other two boys wanted to join him in the ring. They were both too shy, so just shook their heads and hid behind their mum, but I was up for it. I put my hand in the air and said 'I'll do it.' I had started doing gymnastics by then, so when the clown told me to follow and copy whatever he did – handstands, cartwheels, all that stuff – I was better at them than he was and lapped up the applause like a pro.

There were loads of times I'd get up on a stage when I was little and Mum would cringe, wondering what embarrassing words were about to come out of my mouth, although she was quite happy when I won us a family holiday by dancing on stage at a holiday camp. But it still never crossed her mind that I might end up winning something rather more permanent than that and becoming better-known because of it, no matter how many times I entertained a crowd.

In one way or another, Mum has spent the past twenty-three years watching me perform. But she's been a lot more than just a spectator, because without everything she has done and still does for me, I wouldn't have been able to do any of it. I've put her through a lot of stress throughout my life, from when I was young and up to mischief all the time, to when I was older and she had to sit and watch me compete in nerve-racking finals.

before I had won anything in gymnastics, I always that I wanted to do something with my life that make me stand out from the crowd.

There's no doubt in my mind at all, that if it hadn't been for Mum and the way she's supported me, I wouldn't have even been in those finals, et alone won any medals. It's only as I've got older that I've fully realised the sacrifices she made to allow me to do all that, although she'd still say she was only doing what any mother would. In the run up to the London Olympics, though, it really hit me and I used that thought as motivation. wanted to do it for her, to show her that it was worth all the stress and sacrifice because I had been successful.

Even as I got older, moved into my own place and could drive myself to training, Mum still did whatever she could to make sure all I had to worry about was where my kit was and whether I had enough petrol in my car to get to Huntingdon. It's like if you go to work in the morning and you haven't paid the bills or the house is messy – it clouds your mind. When you're training, you can't have those distractions, you have to be completely focused on what you're doing.

Whenever I've been away from home, whether at a competition or a photo shoot, or for something else, I know that when I come back and open my front door, Mum will have made sure there's food in my fridge, the heating has been on and there are clean clothes in my wardrobe. Like I said, she's my guardian angel and I know I still have a lot to do to repay her for everything she does for me – and to make up for the years of chewed fingernails I've given her.

The little boy who once drove his mum crazy, bouncing off walls, breaking bones and never sleeping, has been replaced by a man who I hope is calm, caring and thoughtful, but one who still knows how to have a good time. My coach says I'm an introverted extrovert these days, which means I like my own space and my quiet time, but when it comes to performing I *can* perform. And I enjoy each of those things just as much as the other. I'll happily sit on my sofa at home playing *Call of Duty* for hours one day, and then spend the next day performing in front of a crowd of thousands.

I know how lucky I am to be able to make a living out of doing what I love. After all, gymnastics isn't a sport that anyone gets into to become rich or famous – good luck to them if they do. It's a sport you do because you have a passion for it. But even before I had won anything in gymnastics, I always knew that I wanted to do something with my life that would make me stand out from the crowd. I wanted people to remember me as someone who achieved something worth talking about. I didn't want to reach old age and just fade away without anyone knowing or caring; I wanted to be remembered. And not just for being the problem child from hell. . .

2

Mischief, mayhem and an illegal Afro

School was weird. If you were a little bit different or stood out from the crowd in any way, they didn't like it at all. Doing something that no one else was doing, or just refusing to follow the crowd, meant that in their eyes you were naughty.

But I like to be different. I hate the idea of blending in with everyone else, of being like a sheep that's herded through life, only thinking and saying what people say you should. So all the way through school, I knew I wasn't going to end up stuck behind a desk when I got older. It might be okay for some people, but it would drive me nuts.

Some teachers didn't like that. Mr Chambers was one of those. He took a class called 'Life Skills' that was about choosing jobs for work experience – two weeks when you're sent out to work in the 'real world'. I must have been about 15 at the time when Mr Chambers asked me, 'What do you want to be when you're older?'

Straight away I said, 'I want to be a sportsman.' I was already doing gymnastics and that was where I saw my future.

'You can't be a sportsman,' he said, frowning. So I said, 'Okay, I want to be a stuntman. If I can't be a sportsman I think I'd like to be a stuntman and work in television.'

'You can't be a stuntman. Come on, let's be realistic, what do you want to do? How about accountancy?'

I just laughed. I hated maths, numbers – all that stuff – so accountancy definitely wasn't for me. And neither were any of the other desk jobs he tried to push me towards. There was no way I was going to end up doing something I hated and plodding through life. I knew that for certain.

I also knew that my lack of concentration wasn't doing me any favours with the teachers. It wasn't through choice. I didn't wake up in the morning and think, *I'm going to be a real pain in the arse today*. My ADHD meant I could only focus for about 15 minutes before my mind started to wander and I couldn't take in anything the teacher was saying.

Sitting in a classroom was just so frustrating. I worked as hard as I could and I understood it was important to get good grades, but there were times when nothing would sink in. History was the only subject that interested me really: the Battle of Hastings and stuff like that. But anything else was just a drag.

Some people love to learn; they love to read books. It could be a book on civil engineering or anything, and they'll sit there and get stuck right into it. I just don't get it. It fascinates me because I've never read a book in my life – at least, I've never read through a book from start to finish. The closest I got was with the last *Twilight* book. I have to be completely free from any distractions to sit and just read, otherwise I'll read ten pages then have to flick back over what I've just read because I'll be like, 'What happened, again?'

There were one or two teachers at school who understood me, but most of the time I felt as though they were all against me. Like the time I almost got sent home from school because of my hair.

I used to wear it plaited when I was young, so I never went to school with my hair undone. Except for once when I just hadn't got around to getting it re-plaited and went to school with an Afro. I remember walking down the corridor and some of the other kids laughing. Then I walked past a teacher, and as I did so she reached out and grabbed my hair. Then she yanked it, obviously thinking I was wearing a wig.

I was like, 'Woah, what are you doing?' She said, 'Take it off.' I said, 'I can't, it's my hair.'

'What do you mean?' I pulled at it, showing how firmly and permanently attached it was to my head and said again, slowly this time, 'It's. My. Hair.'

'Follow me,' she demanded, leading me to a table in the school's reception and telling me to sit down and wait there. I did for about half an hour before I finally decided it was pointless. So I got up and went

to my lesson. Otherwise I'd probably still be sitting there. I think she just panicked and felt embarrassed by the situation, but to me it was just another example of how anything different was seen as wrong.

Another thing I didn't like about school was the constant pressure to be part of a group and to try and get in with the popular kids. I was never into all that. I always had lots of different groups of friends – I could be sitting with one group and I'd hear them bitching or gossiping about someone I was mates with, so I preferred to steer clear of anything like that.

Trying to be popular was never something I was into at all really and it's still not – I just wanted to live my life, you know? There was always some mad rush to be part of the next big thing at school, but I just did my own thing, I didn't want to get sucked into a crowd and get peer pressured into smoking or drinking.

I suppose a lot of that came down to the fact that I was never short of confidence, and that, from about the age of 12, I was a lot stronger than most other kids my age.

PE was probably one of my favourite lessons but I was always picked last at football, everyone used to think I was crap at it because I did gym.

Then I'd get on the pitch and start scoring goals; down the pitch, up the pitch, I had powerful legs so I was pretty fast. I played rugby too; I was put in the school rugby team, playing on the wing. I wasn't too happy about it. I never used to understand the game, I just knew you couldn't pass the ball forwards, only backwards, then you had to run and score a try. I used to think, *Why am I on the wing? It's boring.* Then the ball would come to me and I'd be off up the pitch, and no one could catch me.

Mum always used to worry about me playing rugby. She'd say it was a bit rough and that I might get injured. When I was younger, though, she'd really wanted me to try other sports. I'd spent so much time doing gym that she thought I should try something else.

She started taking me to horse-riding lessons in the village once a week, which was okay, until one week she decided I should go for an hour, instead of the half-hour lessons I'd been having. It was a bad move. I went home afterwards and said, 'Mum, I don't want to do it anymore. My bum hurts.'

That was the end of my (very) brief riding career. But the ballet lessons lasted a lot longer. My brother, Leon, who's three and a half years older than me, did well at it and the teacher said he could be a really good dancer. But I used to see it more as an opportunity to have fun.

I was about six years old at the time and the only boy in my ballet class, so whenever the teacher had her back to us, demonstrating a plié or something, I would be messing about, just generally being a little shit. The parents of the other kids, who were sitting at the side of the room watching the lesson, would laugh and without even turning around, the teacher would be shouting 'Louis!' It got to the point where Mum wouldn't even come in and watch; instead, she'd hide behind the door, cringing.

Eventually, I had to give up ballet – and the tights – because I was starting to do gym on a Saturday as well as during the week, and the two clashed. When Mum told the other parents we were leaving the class, she said they were sad to see me go because I had been their weekly entertainment. From a young age, whatever I was doing, it always had to be fun.

As I got older, that fun became more mischievous. And if it was dangerous too, that was even better. There was an indoor skate park in Peterborough called Y2SK8 and a group of about six of us used to go there quite a lot. The other lads would be down there every day after school, but I was only able to skate at the weekends because I was at the gym during the week.

I was pretty good, though. The boys would be working on something all week, looking at a particular ramp and trying over and over again to get it right. Then I'd turn up on a Saturday and ask, 'What you looking at?' They'd point out the ramp and I'd ride it, add in a little twist and pull it straight off. Whenever a trick went wrong the others would panic and

and upside down or head first, but I'd just roll out of it – I always landed on my feet.

Looking back now, some of the stuff we did was pretty dangerous. We'd really go for it, with backflips and big jumps, three metres up in the air. I did hurt myself a few times, so Mum never let me out of the front door without my helmet. Some people thought it was cool not to wear one, but it's not cool when you've got brain damage.

Another supposedly cool thing I never joined in with was the skaters' fashion for wearing their trousers low, so they were hanging down below their arse. My mate Bob did that; he was only little but he used to buy 36-inch waist trousers so they were really baggy and rippled up around his skates. I did the opposite, tucking my trackies into my big thick socks and USD's, which were the skates we used, telling the others that I needed to look after my ankles.

Y2SK8 was the perfect place to hang out; the music was always on and they sold those little microwave pizzas for a pound. You could stay there all day if you wanted, playing pool and skating until nine o'clock at night. We often did.

There was one time we got chased out of another skate park, in Eye, by this girl's dad, because I threw a stone at her. We were there one Saturday, and she started throwing big clumps of mud at us. For a while we ignored her, but the mud was getting caught in our wheels and making us trip over. So I picked up a small stone and threw it at her, thinking it would frighten her off. It caught her right in the stomach – well, actually a bit lower – and she ran off crying.

We thought *Thank God*, and started to clear all the mud off the skate park. Then, out of the corner of my eye, I saw this massive guy running around the corner towards us. He was huge.

'Ruuuuuuun!' I shouted. We were on skates, so we were just gone.

Mum got a knock on her door after that, just one of many she's had about me over the years. Sometimes I got a smacked arse, and most of the time I needed them. I was never really naughty though, just mischievous.

. . . Well okay, maybe sometimes I was naughty.

I had managed to keep the skating a secret from my gymnastics coach, Paul, for quite a few years. But he was always going to find out eventually. That moment came when I went on a training camp to Lyon in France with the World Class Start squad.

I was about 14 years old at the time, and halfway through the trip we had a day off from training, so a group of ten of us went out for the day with a couple of the coaches to do some sightseeing. In the middle of the town square they were holding an event called 'Wanna Do Roll?' One half of the square was set up like a mini skate park for kids, with cones everywhere, little games and instructors to help you round. You could hire a pair of skates and try it all out.

The other half was a proper skate park and every half an hour the professional skaters would come out and show everyone how it was done. I watched them do their stuff, seeing the others go mad over the tricks and flips they could do, and then went to the skate hire stand and got a pair of skates. I went straight to the big park.

It took the rest of the group a few minutes to realise where I was, by which time I'd skated hard and fast to get to the top of the biggest ramp in the park. I stood there and shouted to everyone. They all turned around and looked at me and I saw my coach's face just drop and he yelled, 'Louis, get down. Get down, now!'

All the French people were shouting at me to get down, too. Alright then. I dropped straight onto the ramp, jumped high over the jump box, up onto the next one, landed a 180 and skated back down.

Everyone was saying 'Woah, that was amazing.' Even Paul was smiling. He learnt a lot about me on that trip, because not long after the skating incident we passed a group of break dancers with a crowd around them and Paul joked, 'Go on then Louis, show them how it's done.'

I jumped straight into the middle of the crowd and busted out loads of moves – handstands, air flares – then I walked off. Paul says now that I amazed him with my talent to be able to turn my hand to anything, but I'll always remember the look of sheer panic on his face when he spotted me up that ramp. He wasn't amazed then. He was too busy thinking, *Oh shit, what am I going to tell Elaine?*

Dancing in front of people was something I'd done quite a bit (although it wasn't exactly *Strictly Come Dancing* style) in local clubs on what we called 'Nappy Nights'. They were under-18s nights for 14–17 year olds, where we used to have big dance battles. Some of the other lads were good dancers too, like Aston, who I've known for years and is now in JLS.

I used to have good battles with Aston. Until I'd pull out my gym stuff – flares and windmills – and people would start chanting: 'Backflip. Backflip. Backflip.' I remember one time it was so dark that I couldn't see the floor but I just thought, *Whatever, I'll do it anyway.* Bob says he was worried when he saw my face get close to the floor; I managed to style it out though – just about.

Bob has been a mate since we were at school together. Whenever me or Mum found a spider in the house we'd always call Bob up to come round and get it – we both hate spiders. Last year he left the UK though, for a two-month trip to Australia, which ended up lasting a lot longer than that after he met a girl there, who he has since married.

During the Olympics he would get up at the crack of dawn to watch me compete, and then when *Strictly* was on, he'd watch my latest performance on YouTube every Sunday morning. He even flew back from Australia in time for the *Strictly* final.

He's someone who remembers all the bad stuff I got up to as a kid. I mean, he was probably there for most of it, along with another friend of mine, Sam. We were always out and about doing all sorts – wrestling in the park, smashing golf balls over the A47 to see how far we could hit the ball, playing 'knock-a-door-run' or 'manhunt'.

When it came to knock-a-door-run, we had our favourites, doors we'd always knock on because we knew we'd get chased. One of them was where a guy we called 'goat bloke', lived. This guy owned a goat – that was weird enough to make him a target.

One of our friends got shot at with an air rifle by 'goat bloke''s wife once; she was waiting for us in the bushes and shot him in the elbow. But most of the time we'd end up in hour-long chases with 'goat bloke' in his car and us running up alleyways and diving into bushes to get away.

Manhunt was what we used to play down at the bottom of Mum's road. Me and Sam would set traps for the others by digging a big hole in the patch of grass at the end of the road, and covering it with branches and tying fishing wire between trees to trip them up. Everything was so well thought out; we'd go down there the day before and set it all up, then go all Rambo and hide up trees or in bushes and wait for the others to come. I was sick at manhunt.

If boys now are anything like what I was like when I was younger, then I'm never having a daughter. I remember finding this old mattress once with Sam and trying to set fire to it. It would smoke for a bit and then just go out. In the end we gave up and started walking home.

Then we saw this big black cloud of smoke billowing out from behind a tree. We ran back to the mattress and it was completely ablaze.

Shit, shit, shit. It was right near the main road and all the smoke was blowing over towards it. We thought we were going to cause an accident, so we started trying to wee on it to put it out. It actually worked better than I thought it would . . .

I remember building an immense tree house in our local park with Sam when we were about 13. We'd stroll casually through the village, me carrying a hammer and Sam a big saw. People would look at us and ask, 'What are you doing?' 'Building a tree house,' we'd shrug, as if a pair of tooled-up young boys was nothing strange at all.

We went around collecting anything and everything – old garage doors, bits of old furniture people had chucked away – whatever we needed to make it the best tree house ever. And it was looking so promising, we just needed a few more panels to finish it off. We needed some more wood.

Where does a kid find wood? There were these old, abandoned garages not far from the park, so we prised the wood off the front of them (they were abandoned shacks), put these new bits of wood up, and got in there. It was good – so nice and cosy.

We weren't finished though, we still needed some steps to go up the tree. We had some wood left over so I was sawing and Sam was nailing the steps onto the trunk. Then I heard this noise: click, click, click. And this voice. 'Put. Down. The. Saw.'

I looked up and there was a policeman, standing there holding up his truncheon. Oh shit. 'Sam . . . Sam!'

'What?'

Then he heard it. 'Put. Down. The. Hammer.'

The policeman made us tear the panels down off the tree and hammer them all back up onto the garages we'd taken them from. That resulted in another knock on the door that Mum wasn't too pleased about.

I never struggled to find ways to have fun. Even when I was on my own at home I could create chaos – like the time I burnt a big hole in my bedroom wall.

Me and my mates had discovered that by attaching the red LED brake lights off our bikes to two speaker wires, you could make the lights flash in time to the beat of the music. We'd tried it with slightly bigger lights too, and it had worked even better.

I decided to go even bigger and wire my stereo up to my bedroom light. I took the switch off the wall – without turning off the power – and put the two speaker wires in to try and make my bedroom light flash. Instead, the fuse blew big time, there was a big black hole in my wall and I was covered in bits of plaster and white paint.

Mum never really knew what to expect next when I was a kid, so she worried constantly about where I was and what I was up to; she still does really. But at least now she knows I'll always be on the end of a phone, or if she can't speak to me, then she can usually get hold of my agent, Gab. When I was younger though, she was always nervous if she didn't know where I was or who I was with.

One Saturday before Christmas, when I was about 11, Mum took me to the village Christmas fête. She left me there to play for an hour and said she'd come and pick me up after that. If I wanted to go anywhere else, or come home earlier, she told me to ring and let her know.

She came back an hour later to the place where she'd left me, but I'd gone. She asked around and a group of boys who I sort of knew told her they'd seen me go off with a teenager wearing a hat – someone they hadn't recognised.

She went nuts, calling all her friends and telling them, 'Someone's taken Louis; some boy in a hat.' She even called the police and told them someone had taken her son. She had all her friends out looking for me in the village until one of their sons turned up and asked what was going on.

Mum told him and he said: 'Elaine, Louis wanted to go up to the end of the village where Sam was playing manhunt, so I took him. And I had a hat on; that's why the other boys didn't recognise me.'

I was just a kid; I'd forgotten Mum's warning to tell her if I decided to go somewhere else and that she'd be coming back to get me. Calling the police back to tell them that it was okay, she'd found her son, was probably embarrassing, but it was good practice for when she had to do it again a few years later.

It was just after I'd got my first car, a Volkswagen Polo 2000 that had set me back £1,800, and Mum was worried about me driving it at night. I went out one evening to a mate's house to watch some boxing that was on quite late and hadn't noticed my phone running out of battery halfway through the evening. So when Mum tried to ring me to find out if I'd got there okay and when I would be leaving, it went straight to voicemail. Straight away it was, 'Oh my God, there's been an accident. Something's happened to Louis.'

It got later and later and she still hadn't heard from me, so she called the police, gave them the details of my licence plate and said something bad must have happened to me. They promised to keep an eye out for my car and Mum spent the next hour or so worrying, until I pulled into the driveway at about 2 a.m. with no idea of the state she was in. I walked in through the front door and heard her say, 'Louis, I've rung the police! You didn't answer your phone!' *Oh shit.*

But if there was one thing she never really had to worry about, it was me drinking. I was always the sober one out of my friends and usually the last one to arrive when we were out, as I'd join them after gym. I'd get home about nine o' clock, say 'See ya later, Mum' and be straight back out of the front door to catch up with everyone.

They'd all be drinking by the time I got there. It was hilarious to watch, so I had just as much fun being sober. The thought of getting drunk and going home to my Mum pissed just didn't interest me at all back then, so even though my mates all thought they were cool getting drunk, I'd be like, 'Nah, you just look like idiots.' Peer pressure never really had any effect on me – I was never the type to be bothered by what other people said.

Even if I had been, it didn't look like fun. Whenever I saw people getting drunk, the girls would always end up in tears and people would be sick everywhere. It was funny to watch them, but the thought of throwing up used to put me off. I didn't know back then that you could just have a few drinks and then stop, that you didn't have to keep on drinking until it made you sick.

I've only been ill from drinking once, and it was awful. It was in Russia when I was about 20 and I'd eaten a huge buffet before we started drinking. The combination of food and alcohol was all mixing around in my stomach, so I went up to my room to chill out. I ran a bath, thinking that might help me feel a bit better, and went back into my room to get undressed, but didn't get very far before I fell asleep on the bed. When I woke up a bit later I felt like crap, so sick. I ran to the bathroom but the toilet seat was down. The next option? My still full – and about to get a bit fuller – bathtub. It was disgusting.

I suppose it's quite unusual for a mum to be able to say she's never really seen her son drunk. Mine can tell when I've had one or two, though. She says I become seriously chatty – as in, you can't shut me up.

Even though my mates all thought they were cool getting drunk, I'd be like, 'Nah, you just look like idiots.'

She also knows that once I do eventually stop talking, having had a few drinks means I can actually get a decent night's sleep. I've always been a terrible sleeper, even when I was a baby. Mum says she was lucky if she got an hour's sleep at night. I had a cot but I was barely ever in it; Mum would let me fall asleep on her and then not dare to move in case she woke me up. When Mum told the health visitor I never slept she'd say, 'Maybe it's the milk, why don't you try him on this one?' Then a few months later they'd have the same conversation all over again. I was put on every type of milk there was but nothing worked; they should have added a few shots of rum.

When Mum reached breaking point she would call my nan, who would come round and lie with me until I fell asleep, to give Mum a few hours off. My Nan was Welsh and used to wrap me in one of those big shawls you see Welsh ladies with. She'd put me in it and sling it over her shoulder, so she could get on with her work around the house without needing to put me down.

My sleep hasn't got much better over the years, which can make things difficult when I'm away training or competing. The coaches have learnt that it's better for everyone if I can have my own room; then I won't piss off whoever I'm sharing with when I'm still awake at 2 a.m., but it's not always possible.

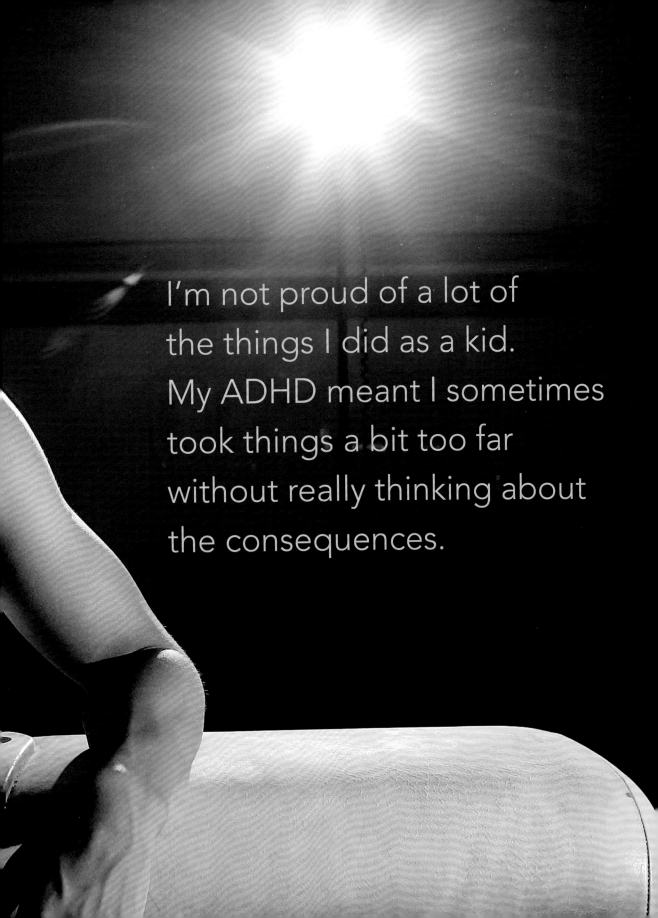

I'm not proud of a lot of the things I did as a kid. My ADHD meant I sometimes took things a bit too far without really thinking about the consequences.

In the early days Mum would tell me to take my headphones away with me and just put them on if I couldn't sleep as the music might help me to drift off. It would make me so envious to see the others who could just get into bed and crash out a few minutes later. I'd be awake for hours while they were in some sort of sleep coma. Even now, no matter how tired I am, I find it hard to fall asleep before the early hours of the morning, and even then I'll be awake again after just a few hours.

There were times when my inability to sleep meant I found other ways to pass the long, boring hours of the night – ways that got me into trouble. There was one time in particular when this was the case. It was at a training camp held at my gym in Huntingdon when I was about 12 and gymnasts from all around the country were invited.

We were all put up in the same hotel near the gym for the whole camp, which my coach Paul was leading. At the end of the first day, he lined all the gymnasts up and told us to let him know if anyone had any problems and which room he was in if we needed him for anything.

Later that night Paul got a knock on his door from a boy who was crying. He said later that before he'd even asked the boy what was wrong, he knew who was at the bottom of it and the boy confirmed it, saying 'Louis is picking on me.' Paul told him it was okay, that he'd speak to me and deal with it at breakfast the next morning.

When Paul called me over to sit with him in the breakfast room I knew I was in trouble for something, I just wasn't sure exactly what. 'Louis, we've got a major problem,' said Paul, his arms crossed, so I knew this was serious. 'You've got to tell me what you've done wrong.'

He sat there waiting while I thought about it. 'Come on, what have you done wrong?' he said.

'Staying up until two o'clock in the morning?' I asked.

'No.'

'Throwing things out of the window in the middle of the night?'

'Er, no.'

'Oh. Banging on everyone's door at midnight or running up and down the corridor?'

'No, Louis.'

'Well, I can't think of anything else.' I shrugged.

'Picking on people!' Paul said, his voice getting louder.

I honestly couldn't remember picking on anyone, but Paul had already decided that because of all the other stuff I'd confessed to, I should be sent home anyway, and called Mum to come and pick me up.

If I'd been fast asleep by nine o'clock I might not have done all those things, but that was me. I never really knew when I was crossing the line.

I'm not proud of a lot of the things I did as a kid. My ADHD meant I sometimes took things a bit too far without really thinking about the consequences. But now that I can look back on those times with a more mature eye, I like to think that now I'm making up for some of those wrongs.

Learning the ropes

My coach, Paul Hall, can't remember the first time he met me. He's being completely honest when he says it wasn't one of those 'light bulb' moments that made him think, *Oh my God, this kid's a future Olympic medallist.* Back then I was just another six-year-old boy being hauled into Huntingdon Gym Club by his exhausted mum, and there were plenty of those. Paul has coached most of them over the years, too, but not all have taken him on quite the same journey as me.

I was about seven years old when I was invited to join Paul's training group, a move that was to have a big impact on both our lives. At the time though, I was just Louis. As Paul himself said, I was nothing exceptional, just a naughty boy who had a habit of being very mischievous.

I remember my first training session in his group quite clearly. Paul introduced me to the other boys by saying, 'This is Louis, he's starting off in the group with us. He's not as good as you guys yet but hopefully one day he might actually be better than you.' I'll always remember that little speech. The others were all older than me by about three or four years, and over time more boys joined and some left, but there was a core group of five or six of us who were always there.

It wasn't very long after I joined Paul's group that Mum came to the gym for a meeting with him. Not because I'd done anything bad – well, nothing *that* bad – but because she had a problem. It was more of a dilemma than a problem, actually. She had a choice to make that would have a huge impact on my future.

Mum always thought I had a good singing voice, so she took me to chorister auditions at the local cathedral school. I remember messing around at the front of the cathedral waiting to be called in, while Mum was busy trying to get me to sit down and behave.

When they called my name, I walked up a huge staircase into a room with a big, long table in the middle. There were about five old guys sitting around it and one other guy by a piano, who gave me a sheet with loads of different songs on it.

'Which one would you like to sing?'

I looked down at the list of songs and shrugged. I didn't know any of them. I asked if I could sing one of my own instead. It was one of the songs we sang at primary school and it had actions to go with the words.

'Shall I do the actions, too?' I asked.

'Just the singing would be fine', said the man at the head of the table. So I sang my song, with no piano accompaniment, just me. I don't think I really understood what it was for at the time, it was just something for me to do and I walked out afterwards not giving it another second's thought.

A few days later, Mum got a phone call from Mr Gower, the choirmaster, who said I'd given such a good audition that they wanted to offer me a place at the school. It would mean I'd get a private education at a really good school, but also that I'd have choir practice every morning before lessons and at weekends too – it was a big commitment.

When Mum told Mr Gower that I was doing gymnastics four times a week, he said I wouldn't be able to carry on training if I did the singing,

I would have to make a choice between the two. Mum didn't know what to do. She knew how much I enjoyed gym, but the chorister position would mean I'd get a really good education that she'd never be able to afford otherwise.

So she came to the gym and we sat down in the coaches' room with Paul. Mum said, 'I don't know what to do. Louis has got a chance for this scholarship to be a chorister but he loves his gymnastics – what should I do?'

'Well, I don't think he's going to get anywhere with gymnastics, but whatever he enjoys the most, go with that – that's what I would do. The only thing I can say is that the position in my training group is a full-time commitment, so Louis wouldn't be able to do both.'

Paul's advice left Mum still hovering between the two choices, so our next stop was my junior school, where I sat in a room with Mum and the headmistress, Mrs Jones. They explained things to me and broke it down into one simple question: Did I want to spend more time singing or did I want to keep doing gym?

'I don't know what to do. Louis has got a chance for this scholarship to be a chorister but he loves his gymnastics – what should I do?'

As a kid I had much more fun bouncing and flipping around, somersaulting and seeing my friends, than standing in a room singing. So as soon as they asked me the question, I said I wanted to do gym, it was much more fun. I didn't want to sing if I couldn't do gym. Some parents wouldn't have let a seven-year-old kid make a decision like that. Some would have said, 'You're gonna have this education. End of story.'

But Mum wasn't like that. She would force me to eat my vegetables and, when I was older, to have a maths tutor, but she wasn't going to force me to stop doing something I loved. Now, I like to think that both of us made the right decision, although it would be interesting to see where I might have ended up if we'd both chosen otherwise, because when I decide to do something, I put 100 per cent into it, and I normally succeed.

In those early days, Paul was quite strict with me, and he had to be. I had a small attention span because of my ADHD, so I was always getting into mischief. Paul would constantly be shouting at me across the gym 'Louis, come here!' or 'Louis, do that.' I got sent out of the gym so many times – so many, I can't even remember what half of them were for. I'm sure it was usually for not listening though. Paul would warn me to be quiet and I'd keep on chatting, having fun, messing around playing hide and seek or hiding someone's gym bag. Finally, he'd lose patience and would say 'See you later, Louis. Get your tracksuit on and go.' So many times.

When he wasn't sending me out of the gym, Paul's way of keeping me out of mischief was to give me new things to do, anything that would keep my mind and body occupied for as long as possible. 'Go and do a thousand of these,' he'd say, or 'Fifty of those.' At first, his favourite punishment for me was the rope, which he'd make me climb over and over again. I'd climb it once, then just sit at the top and mess around, blowing dust off the ceiling.

Then Paul made me start doing pommel horse circles. Whenever I did something naughty he'd say, 'Get over there and do 100 double leg circles.' I was good on the pommel anyway – a bit of a child prodigy – but I did so many more circles and repetitions than anyone else that I became brilliant at it. Paul reckons that by the time of the London 2012 Olympics, I had done one million circles throughout my career – something my old man's body reminds me of on a daily basis.

A lot of gymnasts hate the pommel because it's so hard, but I learned over the years that the more difficult something is, the more you can improve and get better at it. The trickiest thing about the pommel is that the coaches can't support you physically in any way – they can guide you and tell you where to put this hand and then that one, but they can't

actually help you get into positions. That's where it's very unique, and it means that if you do become good at the pommel horse, it's largely off your own back.

I began learning with my legs in a bucket that was tied to a rope suspended from the ceiling, so it was dangling a couple of feet off the floor. You place your hands on a small toadstool-shaped object, called a mushroom. Anchored around eight inches off the floor, it has a large surface to move around making it easier to balance on than the narrower pommel horse. Keeping your feet in the bucket means the weight of your legs is supported, so it's easier to circle and swing them as you would on the pommel. The hard bit comes when your coach takes the bucket away and you're supporting all your bodyweight on your wrists. But to me it never really felt like punishment when Paul sent me to the pommel; it was just another thing to do, another thing to stop me getting bored. I hated doing the rope climbs, but the pommel was entertaining, not that I was ever going to tell Paul that.

During my first few years at Huntingdon Gym, it was run by a man called Terry Sharpington. He started the club in a local school hall in the

'Louis is the one, Paul.
Remember what I say –
he will be your champion.'

1970s with a couple of mats, a vault and a home-made springboard – so the story goes. And he seemed to like me. It was Terry who first told my mum that he thought I would turn out to be one of England's best ever gymnasts. At the time, I don't think she really believed him and even Paul admits that it was Terry who first saw what I was capable of.

When I was about 14, Terry became really ill and sadly passed away, leaving Paul to continue his life's work at the gym. Paul had been to see Terry at home the night before he died and they had spent hours talking and laughing about the best moments they had shared over the past thirty-odd years. My antics came up more than once in their memories of recent times and Terry suddenly looked at Paul in complete seriousness, and told him, 'Louis is the one, Paul. Remember what I say – he will be your champion.'

It was five years later – to the day – that I became the first British gymnast to make an Olympic final since World War II, when I qualified for the pommel horse final in Beijing. As Paul says, Terry wasn't often wrong when it came to gymnastics.

Paul never made a secret of the fact that it was Terry who saw my potential. He had always been concerned that I didn't have the classic build for a gymnast – that my body shape wasn't the normal model for the sport. But over the years I started to change his mind.

It was when I was about 12 that Paul started to think that I was good, that I could achieve something in the sport, though he wasn't thinking in terms of the World Championships or Olympic Games just yet. He wasn't the only one starting to think this. Mum was also beginning to realise that gymnastics could actually be something that would change my life.

It got to the point when, having spent more than four years driving the 52-mile round trip from our house in Peterborough to the gym in Huntingdon three nights a week and every Sunday, Mum sat me down and told me I had another decision to make. She said: 'You've got to make a choice now. Do you want to do gym full time and put everything you've got into it and go as far as you can? Or you can come three days a week – I'll still bring you here – and you can just do it for fun. I'll support you whatever you want to do, but it has to be your choice and you have to put everything into it.'

Just like four years earlier when I'd chosen gym over singing, I had no hesitation in telling Mum I wanted to put everything into the gym. I could be having fun, playing football on the patch of grass at the bottom of our road on a nice sunny day, but when Mum came to call me in to get ready for gym, I never complained or said I didn't want to go. It was one thing in my life that I knew I could really be good at and I loved doing it.

One of the first big competitions I remember going to was the British Championships when I was about 13 years old. At that time the scores in gymnastics were based on the old system, so 10 was the top score you could get. I was competing on the pommel and watched the boy before me go on and do an amazing routine to score 9.65. Paul looked at me, shook me by the hand and said, 'Well, you're not going to win this Louis, because that guy's just done the most amazing routine, but good luck. Just do your best.'

I went up and did my routine, but added an extra element that I'd never used in competition before, to make it more difficult and more stylish. I scored 9.7 and won the competition, but when I walked off the platform Paul looked at me and said, 'What are you doing?' I shrugged. I didn't understand what the problem was.

'Well, I wasn't going to win with my old routine.'

Paul was a bit speechless at that. Gymnasts don't usually take it upon themselves to change a routine at the last minute, especially when they're as young and inexperienced as I was then. It was a moment that made him realise I was a bit different – and a bit crazy too, maybe. But different can be good, it can be special, and Paul knew that. He could see that working with me was going to present all kinds of new challenges and he was looking forward to seeing where the two of us would end up.

The following year gave him a bit more of an idea. Competing at the London Open in March, I finished 6th overall in the senior competition

and topped the junior event. I also got the highest score of the day on the pommel horse – 9.6 – which helped to win me a place in the GB squad for the European Junior Championships the following month, where at 14, I'd be the youngest member of the five-man squad.

I got to train at Lilleshall National Sports Centre – the home of British Gymnastics – to prepare for the competition. It's a place I would become very familiar with over the next nine years or so. Leading up to the London Olympics, they'd always put me in my favourite room if they could, it was one of the few with a double bed so I had space to stretch out properly.

The gym at Lilleshall is about three times bigger than the one in Huntingdon and a lot quieter, too. It's great that Huntingdon is such a buzzing gym and has loads of opportunities for everyone, from young kids just starting out to people with special needs, but at times it did become a bit hard to focus during training.

I'd feel my mind getting very fatigued during afternoon sessions, when all the kids started coming in after school, just at the time when I had to be really switched on mentally. There would be so much going on that it was like trying to do homework with hundreds of kids running around. You'd have to be careful, too; a couple of times when I was practising double somersaults, a kid would suddenly run across my path so I'd have to slam the brakes on before I squashed him.

It was hard to train at Huntingdon sometimes, especially at an intense level. But the staff there definitely have what it takes – as everyone has seen – to make Olympians and Olympic medallists. They've got almost everything the best gym needs; they just need to make it a bit bigger so they can have separate training facilities for the elite athletes and the recreational kids.

At the European Junior Championships in Slovenia, Paul thought I might have a chance of reaching the pommel final, given what I'd done at competitions in the UK over the preceding months. But it was my biggest competition yet and neither of us was quite sure how I would handle the nerves and pressure.

So it came as a surprise to both of us when I won the title. It was uncharted territory; there weren't many European medals for British gymnasts back then. In terms of gymnastics, Britain was not high in the world rankings, so winning medals was not generally something that people expected of us. Paul was stunned when I won, but I like to think I played it quite cool. The BBC spoke to me afterwards for a small piece on their website and I told them something that would become a bit of a mantra for me throughout the rest of my career.

'It's my biggest competition yet and it was very pressurised. I just thought "I've done the training, I'll do my routine and get on with it."'

The big occasion just brought out the best in me; it always has done.

European junior title aside, the trip to Slovenia is probably most memorable for something that happened before the competition had even started. It was the day we arrived in Ljubljana from a warm-up competition we'd been to elsewhere in Slovenia. We checked into our new hotel, put our bags away and then because we had the rest of the day off, we thought we'd go for a walk around the city.

my biggest competition yet and it was very
ssurised. I just thought "I've done the training
do my routine and get on with it."'

There was a group of us waiting in the lobby – which in this hotel was on the fifth floor – for everyone to arrive. Being a little shit and 14 years old, I thought it would be funny if I took the stairs down, pushed the lift button and got in it before they did, so that when they got in the lift I was already in there. As I was running down the steps, I saw this figure falling past the window next to the staircase. *What was that?* I wasn't sure what it was but I had a feeling that something wasn't right, so I turned around and ran back up the steps.

The window at the top was wide open and the bannister that was in front of it had come away from the wall. Everyone was just standing there

by the lift, in shock. 'What's gone on?' I asked. One of the other juniors, a lad called Martin Gordon said, 'Steve just fell out the window.' I was the only one who had the bottle to look over the edge though. We were five storeys up.

Steve was Steve Jehu – a 17-year-old gymnast from Exeter who specialised on the rings and who I'd got to know quite well at the GB training camp in Lilleshall. I went to the edge and looked over. He had fallen onto a little metal corrugated roof on the first floor. He looked so small, I couldn't quite see if he was moving or anything. Then I saw him just turn his head slightly and look up. I shouted 'He's alive. He's alive!'

The seniors were with us on the trip so I ran to one of the senior guys' rooms and knocked on the door. It was Darren Gerrard's room. I banged on the door and as soon as he opened it I spat out the words, 'Darren, Steve just fell out the window.'

'What?'

'Steve fell out the fifth floor window.'

'Oh fuck off.'

I couldn't get him to believe me so I ran to the next room where Ross Brewer was staying – he was the more mature one on the senior team – and told him what had happened.

Ross had just come out of the shower, but he panicked and grabbed this little hand towel, wrapping it around his waist before running straight down to the lobby. He looked out of the window and told me to go and get help. Me and Martin Gordon sprinted down the stairs and went to reception where I told the lady behind the desk, 'My friend just fell out the window on the fifth floor,' but she couldn't understand English. She didn't know what I was saying but she could see I was really panicking, so she went to get a manager who came out and asked, 'What's the problem?' I repeated what had happened and her face went white. I said, 'Excuse me, can you call an ambulance?'

I went up to the first floor, opened the window and climbed out onto the roof where Steve was; Ross was already there, in his little hand towel.

The coaches had gone out for the day too, so Ross rang them and told them to come straight back to the hotel. The fire brigade came, ambulances and the police too.

Steve had landed feet first, which shattered his ankle to bits; it had swollen to the size of an elephant's trunk. But that wasn't the worst of it. The roof he'd fallen onto had support struts underneath which left big steel bolts poking through. After Steve had landed on his feet he'd rolled onto his side and one of the bolts had gone right into his armpit, completely ripping off his skin so it was all hanging down. I was just standing there, staring at him in shock. He looked up at me and said, 'Imagine if someone had that on film.'

The doctor who operated on Steve's ankle said that the 10-metre fall would have killed him if he hadn't put his gymnastics skills to use on landing. Luckily, he was able to leave hospital after a few days on crutches, but if he'd fallen on his head it would have been a very different story altogether. As it was, he ended up winning a silver medal for England at the 2010 Commonwealth Games in Delhi, some six years later.

Returning to Peterborough as a European Junior Champion meant I was, briefly, a bit of a celebrity. Well, I was invited to go on *Blue Peter* for one of my first TV appearances. I remember it quite well; I had my hair in plaits and spoke in this embarrassingly high, squeaky voice. It was good fun. I wasn't really scared of being on TV – you're quite fearless when you're that young – but I was a bit nervous about falling off the pommel during the little display I gave. When they interviewed me after the display they said something like 'Don't be nervous,' and I said, 'I'm not, I'm just out of breath!'

The Athens Olympic Games were on the summer after I won in Slovenia and I remember watching them on TV at home thinking, *Wow, I'm only 15 but I'm scoring the same marks as they are at the Olympics.* I wanted to be there. I was starting to realise that I would have my time, which was exciting, but at the same time you think, *Four years? I've got to wait four years for the next one?* It feels like a lifetime at that age.

Great Britain didn't send a single male gymnast to the Athens Games because the team had completely messed up at qualification in 2003 – I think they finished 23rd – and we'd only sent one gymnast to Sydney in 2000, who was Craig Heap. So I watched bits of the gymnastics from Athens on TV, but there was no one for me to look to really in terms of inspiration, not from Britain anyway. That's why, when I see the kids in the gym watching me now, I like it. It's good for them to see successful gymnasts working, and know that if you train hard you can achieve something.

As I was growing in self-belief, I was also reaching the age when you start to think you know better than everyone. Better even than the coach who has trained you since you were a crazy seven-year-old kid who didn't know his Markelov from his Yurchenko. For Paul, who had always been such a disciplinarian when I was younger, it was difficult to adapt once I became bigger and stronger than him.

Our relationship had to change as I got older and started to argue back whenever Paul tried to tell me to do something I didn't think was right for my training. He says I'm an alpha male and someone who's not afraid to speak his mind, which is probably fair. When I was young, obviously, it was whatever Paul says, goes. But once I had reached 15 or 16 and the hormones kicked in, I would question things more and more.

At the beginning of every session, all the gymnasts would have to line up and listen to Paul tell us what the plan was for that session – that went for the national squad too – and I was always the one who would speak up if something didn't seem right. 'Why do we have to do this?' 'Why are we going here?' Even in national squads with the president and technical director present, I was the same. I suppose I became a bit of a spokesman, and over the years that role continued and developed even more. By the time of the London Olympics, I was looked up to by the other boys as a leader and team captain, which was a great honour and showed just how far I'd come since those days when I'd piss about at the top of a rope in the gym.

But for me and Paul to get to that point involved a big learning curve for us both. Even in the later years, leading up to London 2012, we were still figuring stuff out. Paul has off days, like most people (me included). And when he's having one of those he'll 'go off' at you for the tiniest thing. If I'm guilty of doing something wrong, I'll keep my mouth shut, take my punishment and just get on with it. But if I haven't done anything wrong then I'll stick up for myself. I'll never shout at him, but I'll say something back if I feel I need to.

So we did have our disagreements, right up to the 2012 Games. One that particularly comes to mind was when I was ill. I'd been feeling rough for a couple of days and when I went to the doctor he told me I had a throat infection and gave me some antibiotics. I went to the gym and told Paul, but he was less than sympathetic.

'Why didn't you go to the doctor's sooner, Louis?'

I wasn't feeling good, I had still gone to training and Paul was having a go at me. I didn't want an argument, so I just said, 'Stop, I don't want to be dealing with this today. I'm ill. I just want to come in, do a bit of training and go home.' Then he started shouting and ranting at me, 'Why didn't you do this, you should've gone earlier, now you're ill, you've got this and that . . .'. I just walked out and went home. I wanted to avoid getting into an argument. I was really ill, so I just thought, *I'm going home. I should have stayed in bed – I didn't come to the gym to be shouted at.*

The only thing that was running through my head on the journey home was this: *The reason I go to the gym is for me. I want to train. I want to be successful at the Olympics, I don't need to go there and listen to someone shouting at me.*

I was at the stage in my career when I knew what I needed and how to get it. Over the years I'd learnt that although I might not be the hardest worker out there, I knew what I had to do to get me to the next level and I would make damned sure that I did exactly the right things to do just that.

It was something that I came to realise in the three years leading up to the London Olympics. That was when I took over the direction of my gym career with Paul guiding me, which I think he preferred really. So there were times when I'd go to the gym and know in my head exactly what I needed to do. Paul would have a programme set out for everyone, so at the start of the session he'd say: 'Right, Dan you need to do three of these, ten of those, we'll work on these and hopefully we'll put this into the next competition. Luke, we'll do this and that, etc.'

But in my head I already knew what I wanted to do so I'd say to Paul, 'I need to get squat out full Markelov into my high bar routine,' or, 'I wanna get long swing in my P-bars . . .' And he'd say, 'Okay, go and get on with it.' I'd go off and do it. I'd just do it. If I needed help with something or if Paul saw me doing something wrong then he'd tell me, but most of the time I'd just get on with it.

It was a similar scenario when it came to competitions. When I was young, Paul would have strict instructions for me about preparing. He'd say, 'You've got to do this or that, start an hour beforehand, get yourself ready and get your bag packed.' He'd show us everything in minute

detail. But as the years went by I found my own way to prepare – one that suited me.

It was quite different to Paul's way though, so it took him a few years to get his head around it. Whereas Paul is quite a worrier and he'll get stressed about every little thing, I'm much more laid-back before a competition. There might be 20 minutes to go before a big final and I can be napping on a mat somewhere, until Paul comes and stands over me saying, 'Louis, you do need to get ready now.'

I can always see him getting nervous and twitchy about the fact that I'm so relaxed, which is quite funny. There were times – particularly over the last couple of years – when we'd be at a competition, and I'd leave it until 15 minutes before I was due to perform to get up and have a bit of a stretch. Then I'd go out and nail my routine. Paul says it's unique. I don't know about that. All I know is, it's my way, and it's worked pretty well for me over the years.

4

Turning heads

The date of 6 July 2005 is one that most British athletes can remember pretty clearly because it was the day that this happened:

'The International Olympic Committee has the honour of announcing that the games of the 30th Olympiad in 2012 are awarded to the city of London.'

When I saw Jacques Rogge, the president of the IOC, speak those words to the world, I was sitting in my bedroom at home, just chilling and watching TV before training. On the news they were showing people like David Beckham, Seb Coe and Steve Redgrave going nuts in Singapore, jumping up and down and hugging each other – they looked pretty shocked. There were clips of crowds celebrating in Stratford and Trafalgar Square, too, and I remember thinking, *Wow, this is pretty cool.*

My first thought was how wicked it would be to compete in a home Olympic Games, but I was so young at the time – I'd turned 16 just a few months earlier – and so much more still had to happen before I could even begin to think about that. I'd only won a few junior competitions,

no World Championship medals or anything, so it didn't really feel within touching distance for me. And it was a whole seven years away. In sport, that's a lifetime.

They showed the French bid team crying in the background while Denise Lewis was going mad. Then Seb Coe gave a speech saying we'd won the biggest prize in sport and that hosting the Olympics could change the face of British sport. It was exciting, but I wasn't letting myself get carried away with the idea of being a part of it just yet.

What happened the next day was horrible. It was so weird. The country went from being on an amazing high to complete horror, not even

24 hours later. I was in Peterborough at the time of the London bombings, but I remember thinking how scary it must have been for anyone around London at that time. People who'd just been on their way to work for a normal day in the office were never going to get there – I couldn't get my head around it.

Back at the gym, it seemed the European Junior title I'd won in Slovenia had caught the attention of a few people at British Gymnastics and they decided to select me for the World Championships in Melbourne that November. It felt like everything was happening pretty quickly, but I wasn't complaining; I was gonna get to go to Australia and compete in the Rod Laver Arena – how cool is that for a 16-year-old lad?

I'd had my hair in plaits for a while before then, but it was a style that needed maintaining and I knew I wasn't going to be able to find anyone to do it while I was away, so it was easier to just chop it all off before we left for Melbourne. I do change my hairstyle all the time; I love looking different. I grew it a bit before the London Olympics, then just before the Games started I made a last-minute trip to my barbers in Peterborough, where I've been getting my hair cut since I was 12. I knew exactly how I wanted it and I got so many comments about it during the Games – I never told anyone it only cost me £12.

The team for Melbourne was just me and Ross Brewer – the guy in the hand towel in Ljubljana. He was a very mature guy and very intelligent, the kind of guy who liked to talk about atoms and electrons and stuff. I think he's an accountant now, but even back then he was quite different to me, so there wasn't really anyone for me to hang around with apart from the girl's team. That was okay though, I knew Beth Tweddle, Siobhan Church and Imogen Cairns from juniors, so I wasn't completely on my own.

I know it's a cliché to say so, but I really did go to Melbourne with no expectations whatsoever. I just thought I'd go and do the best routine I could, and see where it got me. As it turned out, I came pretty close to qualifying for a world final at the age of 16. I would have made it if it

hadn't been for one little mistake in qualifying, when I put one hand on top of the other, so that I couldn't take off the one underneath.

It meant that I fell off the pommel, but it wasn't because I was any more nervous than usual, it was just an uncharacteristic mistake. It was an annoying one too, because I could have done so well in that final – really well. I was left feeling frustrated more than anything. Winning a medal at a World Championships would have put me straight up there, and I'd really felt like I wasn't all that far away from a place on the podium at senior level.

I came back from Melbourne believing I could have the same success as a senior that I'd had as a junior, and that was vital to my progress in the months ahead. The qualifying for the 2006 Commonwealth Games – also being held in Melbourne – was getting underway, and it wasn't going to be easy to make the team. I won my second European junior title along the way, which showed I was in good form, but the whole process of qualifying for the Commonwealth Games turned out to be a really rigorous one.

Some senior gymnasts had retired, but there were still quite a few left who were hanging on for the Commonwealths and perhaps the 2008 Olympics, too. So there were all the people my age as well as all the more experienced ones too. And the guy who fell out the window – he was still competing – which meant there were a lot of gymnasts trying to get to the Commonwealth Games. It made it so hard to secure a place in the team.

There were three trial events, with two competitions included in the third one. I pretty much smashed it – every single one. And not just on the pommel, but in the all-around as well. In three of the four trials I think I finished third in the all-around. The 1st, 2nd, 4th and 5th places changed quite a bit, but I was fairly consistent. At the last event, I came joint 2nd with Kristian Thomas, and that pretty much secured my place in the England squad for Melbourne, but it was a really tough process.

I remember two bag-loads of England kit getting delivered to the gym, all for me to wear at the Games. It wasn't like 2012 though where adidas made everyone's kit; the gymnastics stuff for the Commonwealth Games was made by Impsport, who I'd never heard of before. There were loads of different leotards to wear which, when I was young, was enough to get me pretty excited.

I much prefer the cold. I like whacking the heating up, being all cosy indoors and peering out the window to see frost outside.

As was the airport on the day we left. There was a big crowd of us flying to Australia on the same day, from all different sports. I remember it being the first time I'd seen Jess Ennis. She had her javelin in a case and stuff, but I didn't really know who she was at that time, she was just a normal athlete.

The whole thing was brilliant though; it made me really feel like I was someone. When you're a part of something so massive it's like, *Yeah,*

I'm here to compete, I'm wearing an England tracksuit, and there are posters everywhere advertising 'Melbourne Commonwealth Games'. When you're actually a part of it, you feel really good.

I remember getting off the bus from the airport to the athletes' village and it was about 37 degrees. I could feel it burning the back of my neck straight away. That wasn't for me; I much prefer the cold. I like whacking the heating up, being all cosy indoors and peering out the window to see frost outside. I liked Australia a lot but I love home. I love having the seasons, so that it goes from cold to hot. I love opening the blinds to see snow outside. You could never do that in Australia.

Kristian Thomas, Luke Folwell, Ryan Bradley and our team captain Ross Brewer were all part of the team in Melbourne. It was a decent and quite young group and we did well, winning team bronze behind Canada and Australia.

It's funny because people only think of me doing pommels now, but in Melbourne I competed on the parallel bars, high bar and floor, too. At the European Championships, I used to compete on other apparatus as well as the pommels, but because it was never televised people weren't aware of it. I've always trained on everything, but I've not always been the best on everything, which is why you don't see me performing on other apparatus much.

The only pieces of equipment I've stayed away from in recent years are floor and vault because of a knee injury – they're both quite hard on the joints. But it's always been a sensible option to carry on training on other apparatus because it keeps you fit, keeps injuries away, and if someone hurts themselves mid-competition, you could step in and do the apparatus. The pommel has always been my bad-ass piece, though.

When I qualified for the pommel final in Melbourne, I thought I could do well enough to win a medal, but it wasn't going to be straightforward. It was while we were in Australia that I first hurt my wrist – an injury that I've had to manage ever since then. When I had it scanned, they found a cyst on the wrist as well as a stress fracture and a cartilage tear, so it was a real nightmare. It meant I had to change my routine while I was out there because I couldn't twist my arm in a certain way. I couldn't even do that much on it in training, so I was just going to have to go for it on the day.

I knew my main rival would probably be the Australian, Prashanth Sellathurai. I'd competed against him before so I knew how good he was and I thought it would be close between us, but on that day I beat him. It was amazing. I couldn't really explain it then and I still can't now. I remember speaking to the BBC afterwards and all I could say was 'I'm totally lost for words'. A gold medal, at the age of 16 was just . . . Wow.

I didn't know what to do when I went up on the podium to get my medal. I didn't know where to look or if I should be smiling or crying. The whole competition had been so close between us, so for me to win and Prashanth to get silver was just unbelievable.

When I got back from the Commonwealth Games I got a great welcome home from my mum and brother, who hadn't been able to afford to come out to Melbourne, and from my nan. They were all over the moon with my gold medal, and just as shocked as I was. For all of us, there was also a little taste of what was to come in terms of having to do interviews. It takes time to get used to people you've never met wanting to know everything about you, from what music you like to how many girlfriends you've had, and everything in between.

Going back to school was the best part about coming home, though. All the teachers that had given me a hard time and gone on and on at me about prioritising my school work over gym training were suddenly realising that I was actually pretty good and deserved a bit of slack. That felt good. It was like 'Yeah, in your face.'

The reaction from other kids at school was crazy, too. I was like a mini hero. I had my own wall in the school – a Louis Smith wall to say 'Well done', so it was covered in pictures that the younger kids had drawn of me on the pommel or being awarded my gold medal. I was getting a lot of attention from girls, too, but I wasn't really interested in getting a girlfriend for the time being.

I'd seen from watching other people in relationships that they could be a pain in the arse, so I thought I'd wait, just bide my time. I'd been to the Commonwealth Games and there was the World Championships the following year, and then possibly an Olympics after that. I'd started to feel like my gymnastics was actually going somewhere, so I didn't really have time for a relationship.

I was in my first year of A levels by then, taking media studies and sports science. I'd actually not done too badly in my GCSEs, considering I had missed six months of school in my last year. It helped that Mum had forced me to have a maths tutor and do an hour of maths every Saturday. That was my only day off so I did moan about it, but I got a C for maths in the end, which I probably wouldn't have done without the extra help. For someone with ADHD who really wasn't bothered about learning stuff, my grades were pretty good.

When Paul had called me and asked if I wanted to go to the Gymnastics World Cup Finals, I assumed at first that he'd meant as a spectator.

But it wasn't long before I was leaving the country again. In December I was invited to the Gymnastics World Cup Finals in Brazil, which was a huge thing for me, even bigger than being at the Commonwealth Games. The World Cup Finals were only for the top eight performers in the world on each apparatus and I hadn't been on the original list of competitors. So when Paul had called me and asked if I wanted to go, I assumed at first that he'd meant as a spectator.

To be included in the top eight pommel specialists in the whole world was an incredible feeling, so when I went clean and finished fifth I was incredibly pleased. It almost felt like I'd come fifth at an Olympic Games, because I'd been up against people from across the globe.

It was made even sweeter because the changes I'd made to my routine in Melbourne hadn't gone down well with one of the judges in Brazil. He doesn't really like me that much anyway – I don't know why – and after watching my routine in training he told me and Paul that it wasn't worth the right amount of points because of the position of my hands. So I changed the routine back to what it used to be and it ended up being worth more points. He probably wished he'd kept his mouth shut.

At the beginning of 2007, which was three months into my second year of A levels, I was packing for Australia again, this time to compete in the Australian Youth Olympic Festival in Sydney. The Australian Olympic Committee set it up after the 2000 Sydney Olympics as a way of giving young athletes a taste of the Olympic experience. So we got to live in athletes' village accommodation, go through drug testing (learn how to piss in a pot), and take part in opening and closing ceremonies.

It was the first year that Team GB had been invited to send a team and we joined others from the USA, Canada, China, South Africa, Germany and, of course, Australia. There were some other Team GB athletes there who have gone on to become quite well known too, like Tom Daley, who was then only 12 years old. He had to be given special allowance to compete because officially the festival was for 13–19 year-olds. The table tennis player Paul Drinkhall was also there – he's now the British number one – and Aaron Cooke, the taekwondo guy who was the world number one at the time of London 2012, but wasn't selected for Team GB.

It was good fun, but looking back now I can see it wasn't really like the Olympics – there were little kids running around everywhere. It was more like a mini Commonwealth Games. But it was important for me to go and compete because the more competitions I entered, the more exposure I got, and people started noticing when I won and remembering my name. Each medal and each success was another step on the ladder towards the Beijing Olympics and every clean routine I did under pressure would count for me in the selection process.

So winning gold on the pommels, as well as silver in the all-around and bronze on the high bar in Sydney were really valuable results, proving that among gymnasts in my age group, I was the best in the world. Once the festival finished, we had about a week off to spend in Sydney, just relaxing and having a look around. I remember sitting on the beach under a cloudless sky in temperatures of about 30 degrees, eating some fish and chips. But all I could think to myself was that in five day's time I would have to go home and go back to school.

I thought, *Right now, I'm sat here living this life, doing this. Do I really want to go back to that?*

It was a no-brainer. There was no way I was going back. I said to myself: *I'm gonna work my arse off in the gym and get more of this; more big competitions, more medals, and more time to actually reflect on it all.* So I never went back to school. Mum didn't want me to give it up, but I think she could see that I wanted to work hard in the gym and give it everything I could to make it a success. The only reason I'd stayed on at school in the first place had been to please Mum. I don't think she realised how stable an environment the gym could be, so she had really wanted me to stay at school. That was sensible, but it got to a point when I had to focus on gym completely, and I couldn't do that while also studying.

Not everyone was convinced though. There were some people who were still stuck in the mindset that a British gymnast would never be able to compete with those from China or Eastern Europe where more time and money is thrown at the sport.

I remember having meetings with the bosses of British Gymnastics ahead of the 2007 European and World Championships – the latter being really important in terms of qualification for the Beijing Olympics. The whole GB squad met with the head coach and technical director, so they could get an idea of what we wanted from the sport.

I don't care which Olympics I do it at, but I want to win an Olympic medal.

They sat us down and talked about the upcoming competitions and how we saw ourselves progressing. 'What do you expect from yourself? What do you want to do in the sport? How far do you want to go?' I was crystal clear on all those things. I said, 'I want to go to Beijing and the London Olympics.'

'Okay, what do you want to do when you're there?'

'I don't care which Olympics I do it at, but I want to win an Olympic medal.'

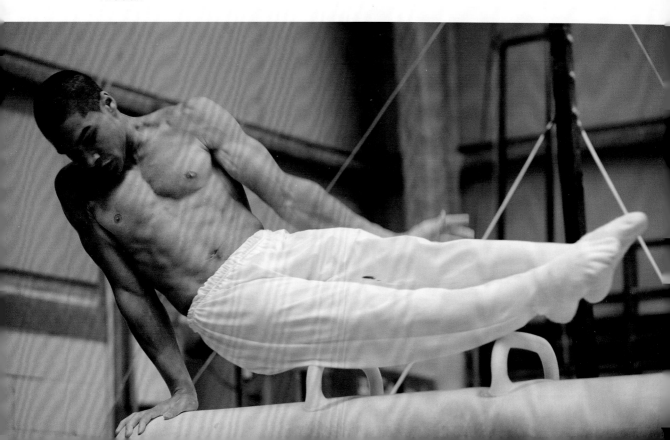

They laughed. That was their mentality: No one has won an Olympic medal for eighty years, so don't start thinking you can win one now. Well, they're not laughing now, are they? It didn't make any difference to me at the time. I've never been the type to listen to what other people think I can or can't do – I know what I'm capable of. Even back then, I knew.

A few months after the Youth Olympic Festival I was packing my bags again, this time for a trip to Amsterdam and the European Championships. And in qualifying it seemed like my full-time gym focus was paying off. I had the third highest score of everyone on the pommel – 15.725 – so was safely through to the final. Paul was happy too, seeing it as another tick next to my name in terms of Beijing, plus the final was taking place on his birthday so it was looking like a great day.

I couldn't quite deliver a medal as his birthday present, though. In the final I messed up on one of the most difficult elements of my routine, and it cost me. I ended up finishing 4th with 15.300, but my teammate Dan Keatings did really well and won silver with 15.450, so at least Paul had that to celebrate. As for me, I just put it down as one of those competitions that remind you how expensive one small slip can be.

I knew I'd need to perform better in finals leading up to Beijing if I was going to make it to my first Olympic Games. I also knew that being a full-time gymnast meant there were no more excuses. I started to spend less time messing around with my mates and more time training hard. I mean, I was still me, having a laugh around the gym and making it enjoyable. I don't think I'll ever be your typical focused athlete who does everything 100 per cent right all the time, but I was definitely starting to understand that the more I put into gymnastics, the more I'd be able to get out of it.

And with me and Dan both winning medals, it was clear that whatever the bosses at British Gymnastics thought, we were definitely on our way up in the world. Stuttgart was where we'd find out a lot more about how far we'd come and how far we still had left to go. It was where the 2007 World Championships were being held and we'd need to do well there if we were to qualify for any of the men's spots at the Beijing Olympics in 2008.

The team for Stuttgart also included Kristian Thomas, Luke Folwell, Ross Brewer and Danny Lawrence. All six of us had the same aim – to avoid a repeat of the World Championships in 2003, when the men finished 23rd, and we had no qualifiers at all for the Athens Olympics. We knew we were better than that but we still had to prove it.

I performed on four pieces in team qualification: parallel bars, vault, high bar and the pommel horse. I scored well on all four but I absolutely nailed my pommel routine, scoring 15.825. That, together with Dan's 15.675 on pommels, helped us to the third highest total of everyone on that apparatus. The other boys performed well, too, and we finished in 15th position, securing us two individual men's places at the Beijing Games. Job done, as Paul said.

But there was still the pommel final to come, which both Dan and I had qualified for, in 4th and 3rd places respectively. The chance to take on six of the best pommel workers on the planet was exciting for both of us, and for Paul, who had us in the gym training hard in the days following the team qualification.

On the day of the final we caught the lunchtime bus to the competition venue, and I was feeling good. It was the first time Mum had been able to watch me compete in a major championship and she had a seat about three rows back from the front, so when we marched out for the final I could see the nerves written all over her face. She looked petrified. I managed to pop my head over the security barrier a couple of minutes before my routine and told her to just chill – if I wasn't scared then she shouldn't be. It was only ten years' worth of work coming down to the next 50 seconds, after all.

My self-trickery worked, and I held my nerve to score 15.600 and win a bronze medal, my first World Championship medal and the first medal won by a British man at a gymnastics World Championships in thirteen years. I just remember being shocked, jumping up and hugging Luke

who was watching from the front row. It was massive for me but it was also massive for the sport in Britain. No one expected it.

I had believed I was capable of winning a medal in Stuttgart, but I wasn't expecting it to happen because I knew how tough it would be.

It's actually harder to win a World Championship medal than an Olympic one because there's no qualification process to get there, so there are more competitors at the Worlds – everyone is there.

The medal ceremony took place in the main square and there were thousands of people there watching and asking for autographs afterwards. I loved it and I knew it was a huge step for me towards Beijing. Even though the two places we had secured for the Games could have been for anyone (they counted as Olympic 'visas' for any male GB gymnast), and we wouldn't know for sure who had them until a couple of months before Beijing, getting that medal in Stuttgart was crucial. I still had to prove myself in the competitions that would follow, but I knew that if I could win a medal at a World Championships, then I could do it at the Olympics.

It was after I got back from Stuttgart that I felt the time was right to do something I'd wanted to do for years – get a tattoo. I wanted something that had some meaning, not just something tacky that I'd end up being embarrassed about in a few years' time. I wanted something that would kick me in the backside, something I'd always remember at those times when my body was hurting and my brain just wanted to play PlayStation all day.

I ended up getting a cross at the top of my back with angel wings coming off it and the words 'What I Deserve I Earn' written over the top. I don't even know where it came from, I just thought of it. It felt like a good way of explaining that what you put into life, you get out – a sentiment I think is really important and one I already know I'll share with my kids as soon as they're old enough to understand.

I suffered for it, though. I remember going to this parlour in Peterborough and it being an absolute nightmare. It was the most painful few hours of my life; my arms were shaking and I had sweat dripping off my forehead.

They had to shut the door so no one could hear the noises I was making when the tattooist started going over my shoulder blade.

It's a weird pain; it feels like someone's sticking a knife into you and dragging it along your skin. The guy did one little line of the cross and I said 'Are you done?' He was just laughing at me and then at the end of it he gave me this card, which said something like 'I got my first tattoo here and I was a complete wimp.' Which is probably true, but oh my God, it was so painful.

I had told Mum beforehand that I was going to get a tattoo done but she didn't know what I was going to get. She liked it though, and she likes the ones I've had done since then as well. She's not a fan of tattoos generally, but she's not against them if they actually mean something, which all of mine do.

Winning a medal at world level was obviously great for my self-belief, but it also meant I received a boost in funding at the beginning of 2008, which was so important in allowing me to give everything to the sport. Sometimes people think that because you're winning medals and your name is in the papers every now and again, it means you're making loads of money. But I'm a gymnast, not a footballer; we don't make hundreds of thousands of pounds a week. In fact, at the time I won a World Championships medal, my funding from the Lottery was about £300 per month.

I was supposed to go straight on to podium level funding after Stuttgart, which would have given me £26,000 per year and really helped me and Mum pay for travel to training, and everything else you need to train full time. But then I received a letter saying that if you were under 25 – which I was – then you only got junior top level funding, which was about £18,000 per year.

I didn't really understand that – how can you age-categorise funding? It was so frustrating. I wanted to write them a letter. If you're a footballer then I can sort of understand it, because you have a ten-year lifespan in the sport, but my career could end before I'm 25 and I wouldn't even have received enough support to fund my own training or to move into my own place.

In the end, they gave me the full amount, but there were plenty of top gymnasts at Huntingdon who were left to get by on peanuts.

I remember Luke Folwell who was really talented and trained twice a day, Monday to Saturday. He was on about £200 a month at the age of 21. It makes it a lot harder to concentrate on training if you're worrying all the time about how you'll pay the bills or manage to put petrol in your car to get to the gym.

The year came to a successful end for me with gold on the pommel at the British Championships and silver at the Glasgow Grand Prix, but I was still playing the waiting game; you can never assume anything when it comes to team selection. Especially when you mess up a routine the month before the squad is announced, which is exactly what I did at the 2008 European Championships in Lausanne.

It was May 2008 and our juniors had done amazingly well – Dan winning the all-around junior European title and Dan Purvis, who was only 15 at the time, winning silver just behind him. Kristian Thomas was doing well too, making the floor final. And me? I was only 5 seconds into my pommel routine in qualifying before I fell off. I got back on and finished my routine, but that was it, I didn't make the cut for the final.

It was just a small mistake, but it had knocked me off balance before I could correct it. I hadn't fallen at a major championship since my first Worlds in Melbourne in 2005, so when Paul said, 'These things happen,' all I could think was, *But why do they have to happen now? Why not six months ago?* It didn't help that Mum had already scraped together enough money for her flight to Beijing.

The next few weeks weren't much fun but there was nothing I could do, except sit and wait. When the phone call finally came it was a huge relief but it was also madly exciting. I was going to my first Olympic Games – the biggest stage a gymnast could ever hope to perform on. The years of hard work in the gym, the bodily aches, pains and strains had not all been for nothing. This was my chance to prove that what I earned, I deserved.

5

History boy

When I think back now to my life before the Beijing Olympics, it's almost like I'm talking about a completely different person – one with no sponsors, no gold medal expectations and a social life that revolved around Pro Evo nights at home with my mates, instead of getting 'papped' on a night out in London.

Inside the gymnastics world, people knew who I was, but I wasn't really a household name like Beth Tweddle – everyone knew who Beth was. I preferred that though, because it meant I could kind of scoot under the radar a little bit. I did do some interviews before the Games, but nothing like the amount I've done in recent years.

And in the interviews that I did do, I played the whole situation down. I said it was a stepping stone for 2012 or that it was more about getting experience of an Olympic Games for me than anything else. At the back of my mind though, I was thinking that I'd just won a medal at the World Championships (in Stuttgart) and that this Olympic Games would be easier than the Worlds – well, there'd be less competition. So I had got the potential to win an Olympic medal.

But I never once said it out loud, to myself or to the media, just to try and avoid any of the stress or expectation it would bring. Although I knew in the back of my mind it was possible, I never said it, because I knew that I'd be asked about it all the time, 'Are you going to Beijing to win gold, Louis?' I'd have enough of those questions in the years to come.

'Are you going to Beijing to win gold, Louis?'

Because we hadn't done well enough to qualify a whole GB men's team, we could only send two British male gymnasts to compete in Beijing. To be picked to fill one of those two places was amazing. It made me feel that those fifteen years of hard work in the gym were finally starting to pay off. And Dan Keatings was the other gymnast selected, which was cool because we both trained with Paul at Huntingdon and were good mates.

I still remember how excited we were when we went to pick up our GB kit for the Games. We had to go to this huge warehouse in Birmingham with Beth Tweddle and the rest of the girls who were going to Beijing. That was the first time I got the proper kitting out experience and it was kind of like going shopping, walking out of Next and into Topshop, from one shop to another, and just trying on everything. Then people made a note of what you wanted – yep, this one, that one.

Finally, you came to a desk where there were bags and bags of stuff packed, ready for you to take home. It wasn't just clothes, either. You got things like a camcorder, headphones, all sorts of gadgets and stuff. It was brilliant, I love freebies – everyone loves freebies. I ended up with so much stuff after the Games that I couldn't fit it all in my wardrobe, so most of it I signed and gave to charity and other bits I gave to my friends.

I'd never been to China before and I remember having to do all these thumb scans and stuff when we got there, which I thought was quite weird. There had been loads of stories in the news before we left about how polluted and smoggy Beijing would be, and they were saying some events might even have to be postponed if it got too bad. So when we left the airport on a bus to the athletes' village I was expecting to get stuck in queues and queues of traffic.

But there was nothing, no traffic on the roads at all. We drove along this really straight, long road from the airport to the village and it was just dead, like a scene from those zombie films where you're the only person left alive. It was quite strange.

When you go somewhere you've never been before to compete – like Beijing – you never really feel like you get to experience it properly, because as soon as you get there, you're in competition mode, especially at an Olympic Games. So you don't get to the Olympic Village and think, right, let's go and have a look at this or that. You get there and it's right, unpack, get down to have some food, early night, training tomorrow at eight in the morning – it's all very regimented.

And the village was obviously packed with athletes from all over the world so there wasn't much of a Chinese feel to it at all, apart from the helpers, or Gamesmakers as they were known in London. The place was just perfection, though. To get from our apartment to the food hall we could either use the main path or we could walk through the gardens, which were just beautiful. There were ponds and paths running all around them.

There was an island in the middle of this massive lake with a bridge to it and stepping stones. And in the water there were loads of Koi Carp swimming around – it was stunning. The ponds in the London Olympic Village were green, so they had people in big wellies fishing out all the algae. Don't get me wrong, the London village was better in other ways – it was right next to Westfield shopping centre for a start – but Beijing was beautiful.

Even in the food hall it was hard to really get much of a feel for Chinese culture. At any big multi-sport competition the food options are pretty similar, because they try to cater for everyone. So they had cuisines from all over the world in Beijing, as well as the burger places you have to avoid until you've finished competing. It can be tempting to try everything, but you'd be surprised how focused you get when you're there, so it didn't really interest me at all. It's strange, because as soon as you finish it's like 'Where are the cheeseburgers? Get me some bacon!'

No one was really expecting anything of me, I was just gonna go out there and have fun.

Mum had managed to get flights out to Beijing with help from my nan and her aunt, but it wasn't easy in those days when I was only on a bit of lottery funding and couldn't really help out with the cost. She also had to arrange for my uncle to come and look after Nan while she was away, so there was a lot for her to sort out, but she was determined to come and watch me in Beijing.

Luckily, with Dan also qualifying, his parents could travel out there with Mum and the three of them rented an apartment about an hour and a half outside Beijing – it was too expensive to stay any nearer. It meant they had to get about three trains to the National Indoor Stadium where the gymnastics was being held, which was hard for Mum, but she was only worried about watching me perform; she never puts herself first.

The first and biggest challenge I faced in Beijing was qualifying for the pommel horse final. The format is always the same at the big competitions – everyone has a chance of qualifying for the final, so you're up against a lot of good gymnasts. Once you're in the final, there are only eight of you and anything can happen.

In qualifying, I went for my easier routine, which was still harder than most other people's. My aim was to do a clean routine and then just see what happened. I did exactly that, nailed it, and qualified in 5th position for the final in eight days' time. It was such a great feeling to have held my own among so many top gymnasts at my first Olympics. Dan didn't make it through to the pommel final, but he qualified for the all-around final and finished 20th, which was a brilliant start to his Olympic career.

I went into the final with the mindset that I'd already done the hard bit by qualifying. So although it was the Olympic final, no one was really expecting anything of me, I was just gonna go out there and have fun. I've always prepared myself for pressure situations like that; I trick myself into believing it's not that big a deal and that there is no pressure because there are no expectations. It's something that worked for me all the way up to London 2012, when there was no way even I could ignore the billboards with my face splashed over them and the expectations of ten different sponsors.

Taking the pressure off myself was something I just started doing quite naturally as a kid. I've never worked with a sports psychologist and Paul never felt I needed one. He has a theory that the people who need a sports psychologist are the people who need lifting a little bit more, not the people like me, who he says have an innate ability to be able to perform.

I did go to one talk by the British Cycling Team sports psychologist, Dr Steve Peters, a couple of years before the London Games. It was part of an adidas event that they were putting on for their sponsored athletes, to help them understand and prepare for what London would be like. But when he started talking about controlling your 'inner chimp' I knew it wasn't for me. It's obviously something that has worked well for people like Sir Chris Hoy and Victoria Pendleton, but I don't think it's the same for gymnasts.

In the week before the pommel horse final in Beijing, me and Paul had seen the world champion, Chinese gymnast Xiao Qin, in training, and noticed he was using his easier routine. We both decided right then that my best option in the final would be to go all out and do my more difficult routine, which had been going really well in training. It was worth two tenths more in points than the one I'd done in qualifying, so we knew that if I pulled it off, it would give me a chance of winning gold.

In the warm-up gym on the day of the final, I was doing my usual thing of trying to stay chilled and messing around to lighten the mood. The warm-up gym is the most nerve-racking place before an Olympic final, because everyone is looking at what everyone else is doing, to see if their routine is better or who might be the one to watch out for. And in Beijing the gym was on a raised podium, so you felt even more like you were on display.

I could see Paul getting more and more tense, so when he nipped out to go to the loo I decided to play a trick on him. When he came back I was gone, and he started running around looking everywhere for me, as we were just about to march out for the final. As he leaned back against the podium, scratching his head over where I could be, I reached out from underneath it where I'd been hiding and grabbed his leg. 'What are you doing?' he shouted, before telling me to get my shit together 'Right now!'

Paul knows I'm quite an extrovert anyway, but over the years he's seen that when it comes to a final or a stressful occasion at any major event, I get even more loud than usual. On the bus I'll put my reggae music on and sing, or play tricks and just be generally buzzing. Everyone else will be nervous and quiet while I'm the opposite, but Paul knows now that the noise is just my way of dealing with the nerves.

I was sixth to go in the final in Beijing, so went out and sat on the arena floor with my coat over my head, trying to concentrate on my routine, listen to the arena and feel the atmosphere. I saw the American who went before me fall off. That was one down.

My routine was solid. There was no way I was going to fall off, but I did split my legs slightly which cost me marks. When I landed that routine though, I was close to tears. Although I wasn't perfect, I raised my arms and shut my eyes because I'd never had a feeling like that before.

When I landed that routine, I was close to tears.

It was so emotional. I'd thought it would just feel like competing in a Commonwealth Games or World Championships but it was another level completely.

Walking back down the steps towards Paul, I was overwhelmed by that feeling of 'Aaahhhhh, I've done it', because it had been so nerve-racking. Deep down I'd been so scared, so the feeling of relief – of satisfaction – was incredible.

When the scores came up I was in the silver medal position. But there were still two gymnasts left to go, who could have possibly pushed me out of the medals altogether. When the Venezuelan guy who was after me fell off it hit me, *Shit, I'm guaranteed a medal.*

Then it was the Croatian Filip Ude's turn and he got the same score as me, but with an easier routine. When the scores are tied, the decision goes to the gymnast with the better scores for execution, which was Ude. So although I'd done the hardest routine of anyone in the final, I got bronze, not silver.

Deep down I'd been so scared, so the feeling of relief – of satisfaction – was incredible.

Not that I was fussed at the time, though. I was 19 years old, at my first Olympic Games and had just won my first Olympic medal. Fifteen years of hard work had all been worthwhile and it had given me the taste for more. I could see Mum in tears in the crowd, and even Imogen Cairns, one of the other gymnasts, was crying.

I wasn't even aware of what I'd done in terms of Olympic history – that I was the first British male gymnast to win an individual medal in one hundred years – until the media started bringing it up in the mixed zone afterwards (where the athletes meet the media after an event). The last medal winner before me was Walter Tysall who had won all-around silver at a time when the rope climb was included. The rope climb!

The reporters seemed to have all the facts and information and were keen to talk about it, but I hadn't a clue. I couldn't really take it all in. At that point, it was still just little old me and Mum. There were no sponsors, no agent. I was just a teenager from Eye so to have done that – made history – was a strange feeling.

I managed to see Mum briefly after the mixed zone but everything got very hectic very quickly after that. I was wanted for loads of interviews and people were coming up to me asking for pictures and autographs. It was all very surreal.

The night after I won my medal, me and Dan decided to go out for a few drinks. We'd heard a lot of people talking about a place called Heineken House and decided that we'd go there when we'd finished competing, so that was where we headed. We went for a meal first, so it was late by the time we got there and the place was maxed out, they wouldn't let any more people in.

We stood outside for a bit wondering where to go and there was a big group of English people there doing the same thing, so we got chatting to them. Some of them were in China working for Omega and one, a guy called Gab, was an agent. I was quite pissed at the time but I remember talking to him. He asked me if I had an agent and I said no, but that people

were telling me I should get one. We ended up going to a rooftop bar in Beijing with everyone else until six or seven in the morning and at some point in the evening we swapped numbers. Gab gave me his card and said he could get me a meeting a few days later with adidas. And he did, so then I thought, *This is a man who knows his shit.*

It's funny how things work out. Gab had first read about me on the plane to Beijing. There was an interview with me in the British Airways magazine, which was ironic as it was probably two years later that British Airways sponsored me, and it's been a great relationship together. In the interview, there was a shot of me on the pommel wearing a striped T-shirt with a bit of an Afro. I think I just stuck in his head. When he was out there and heard that I'd won a gymnastics medal he thought I'd be a guy worth chatting to. And just few days later we met, quite by chance.

We went to meet adidas a few days later to say 'Hello' and show my face in their hospitality area. I didn't really know what it was all about in Beijing, unlike at London 2012. By then, I knew that after the award ceremony, you go down to your sponsor's area and say 'Hello' to the bosses, so they can congratulate you and look at your medal. But back in Beijing, I remember sitting in this room with Denise Lewis and some other athletes I recognised. It was crazy. Only three days earlier, no one in that room would have known who the hell I was.

I stayed in touch with Gab after Beijing and he got me bits and pieces of work with a few different brands. He was really keen to sign me up so he went to Lilleshall to meet with British Gymnastics and also to the gym to meet Paul, just so they could see who he was and what plans he had for me. British Gymnastics called him back a few weeks later and said they were going to advise me against signing with an agent. Paul disagreed. He told me it was a good opportunity to make the most of my success, but that I should make the decision I felt was right.

I was edging towards signing with Gab when he called me to ask if I wanted to present an award at the MOBOs. *Whaaaat?* I was so excited. I'd never been to a proper awards night before and I was being given the opportunity to present an award with Alesha Dixon, so that pretty much sealed the deal. Since then Gab and I have become really close – I couldn't have dealt with the madness in the lead up to 2012 and afterwards without him.

The flight back from Beijing was something pretty special too. All of Team GB was on it, so the atmosphere was brilliant, and when we landed at Heathrow there were masses of people and press waiting. It was even weirder when I got back to Eye in Peterborough; the village was decorated with banners and balloons and people were lining the streets near Mum's house. I went straight to see Nan first and then on to my local where there were about a hundred people waiting – all wanting to see the medal and talk about my Olympic experience.

I was the first British male gymnast to win an individual medal in one hundred years.

What with training and preparation camps before the Games, by the time I got home I'd been away for nearly six weeks. I thought a holiday with my friends would be the best way to chill out and catch up with them, so I booked a caravan in Great Yarmouth for a group of us. I thought it would be good to go somewhere that was a bit out of the way – I didn't think many people would know who I was in Great Yarmouth, so I could just relax there. It was September by the time we went. It was too cold for the beach, but we had a great week of going out, having fun and just chilling. It was quite different to the holiday I took in Marbella after the London Olympics, but just as good in different ways.

I went back into training for a Grand Prix event in Glasgow as soon as we got back from Great Yarmouth, but things outside of the gym were changing fast. I was invited to do lots of shows and pommel horse displays at various dinners and events, which was a whole new world to me. I went to one with Paul that was at the Dorchester in London's Mayfair; it was a fundraising event with Prince Philip and loads of celebrities.

I remember being in the green room backstage where everyone was preparing to do their thing – there were comedy acts, jugglers, a guy doing tricks with a football, and I was going to do my pommels. Paul remembers everyone in the room training like mad to get ready to do their stuff before Prince Philip, and I was just asleep on a sofa in the corner, with everyone looking at me, going 'Who's that?'

Paul woke me up just a few minutes before I was due to go on. I yawned, had a stretch and did a few circles on the horse then went out and did my thing. Prince Philip loved it and I got the loudest cheers of the night. When I went back to the green room everyone was like, 'Wow, how does he do that?'

That sort of stuff had been fun just once in a while, but after Beijing it really kicked off. I was at events every week, meeting loads of different people. To start with, it was nice – it's always nice to have people paying you compliments and saying how much you've inspired them, or their little boy or girl, to get into gym. But when I realised that this was how my life would be from now on, that it could never go back to what it was like before Beijing, that's when I started to struggle.

My life had changed completely and it was something that I was finding incredibly tough to handle. Before Beijing I wasn't anyone. I'd spent nineteen years living my life exactly the way I wanted. Then, after Beijing, I was someone completely different and suddenly I couldn't live my previous life any more.

It felt as though the last nineteen years of my life had just been a lie and I was being told, this is your new life now, deal with it. I didn't know where to go or what to do. It was all completely new. I was only 19, so it wasn't as though I was 30 and prepared for it, with a house, wife and kids, and everything was stable. I'd just hit 19 and was about to start going out partying and meeting girls, and then all of a sudden I'm this role model.

I had kids coming up to me telling me I was amazing. I had parents coming up to me telling me I was brilliant; their son did this or that; would I sign this? It was just crazy. It felt like one of those horror films, where you're standing in a hotel lobby and the room in front of you suddenly starts to stretch out and becomes a long corridor – it was as though my old life was at the end of it, getting further and further away.

I didn't know how to handle it. Every day I'd walk out of the front door with a smile on my face and everything was fine. I'd be meeting hundreds and hundreds of different people every week at events and smiling like everything was fine. Then I'd get home at the end of the day and think, *What the fuck has just happened? Who have I become?* It was very depressing.

My life had changed completely and it was something that I was finding incredibly tough to handle.

I didn't want to do anything, or talk to anyone. It got to the stage when I didn't even want to leave my room. I just wanted to be normal and go out with my friends without people coming up to me all the time, or having to worry about being seen having a few drinks. I remember my brother Leon taking me out to a pub further away from where we lived and there were still girls coming up to me asking for autographs and pictures.

I had been in a little bubble before Beijing and now I was being yanked out of it and thrown into what people were telling me was the real world, where you get criticised for saying the wrong thing, or just because someone has decided they don't like you. It's a scary place to be, especially when you're 19 and had no idea it was coming.

Paul would tell me I had to be careful now I was in the public eye; that I couldn't go to clubs and get drunk; that I couldn't be normal. He told me that this was the sacrifice I had to make, this was fame. I was trying to handle it all on my own, but gradually I realised there was someone who could help, someone who could make things seem less scary and lonely.

Her name was Billie Whyatt and we'd known each other since we were kids. We grew up in the same village and our mums knew each other so

we used to play together. When we were at school people used to tell me that she liked me, but I wasn't interested in girls and relationships in those days. I was too busy focusing on the Olympics and gymnastics. I do remember kissing her once though, when we were youngsters, as you do, but nothing really came of it.

But after Beijing, we started to see more and more of each other. It was so nice to be around someone who'd known me before everything that happened in Beijing. She helped me to get through those difficult times after the Olympics, not necessarily by sitting talking about it for hours, but just by being with her – being around Billie made me feel better.

With everything that was going on in my life, it wasn't long before I started to feel like I needed my own space – like I needed to move away from home. I'd come back after a hard 10-hour day at the gym and Mum would be moaning at me about this or that as soon as I got through the door – the usual little things that everyone's mum gets on their back about. Then my brother would be in my wardrobe taking clothes out that I'd not even worn yet; I felt like I had no privacy any more.

Mum cried her eyes out for days after I left.

It had been in my head for a while that I needed to find my own place, but I hadn't done anything about it. Then I remember having this big argument because someone had drunk all my Mountain Dew from the fridge. It sounds stupid but it really pissed me off. I flipped and said, 'That's it, I need to move out. I want to be gone by the end of the week'. I wanted to have my own place so that when I came home, it would just be me. I would have peace and quiet and there'd be no one there to annoy me.

Mum cried her eyes out for days after I left; she says it broke her heart. I wasn't far away, though. I found a little one bedroom flat just a few minutes from her house that I made really nice and cosy. And she'd be round all the time with bits of food and stuff – I'd often get home from the gym to find the fridge full of goodies. I suppose all mums find it hard when their youngest leaves home, but I think mine is still getting over it now.

By this time, Paul had become more than just a gymnastics coach to me, he'd become a bit of a life coach as well. We'd talk about all sorts of things – girls, money, houses. I might not have always taken his advice, but it made training sessions more interesting. I think by then he'd started to see that I knew as much about pommel as he did, and I knew how my body was feeling and what it was capable of, so in training sessions he'd take a bit of a step back. He'd still be there to guide me, but in a different way from when I was younger and needed someone telling me what to do all the time.

We did talk about the 2012 Olympics, and with Beijing out of the way, we could really focus on what it would take to win a medal in London. The scoring system in gymnastics changed in 2006, which means there is no longer any such thing as the 'perfect 10'. Until the change, a score of 10.0 had been the highest possible mark but now it is possible to go higher as the routine becomes more complex. One panel of judges will start with 10 marks and take off deductions for poor execution and technical errors while another panel will evaluate the 10 most complex elements in a routine and use that to give it a tariff or difficulty rating. The final score is a combination of both the execution mark and difficulty rating.

It means that gymnasts who can do the really difficult stuff have more of an advantage, which Paul was always convinced benefited me on the pommels. My execution might not always be the cleanest, but he knew I was capable of doing the most difficult routine in the world, so we started to put it together.

The idea was to find the best combination of skills that would give me the highest score. Once we had it, we would keep adapting it, slotting in extra elements every year to take it even higher. So by the time London 2012 came around, I had three or four different options when it came to my routine. I had a safe option, which would earn me a maximum possible score of 6.7 for a perfectly executed routine, then a 6.8, 6.9, 7.0 and 7.1, which is very close to the theoretical ceiling of what can actually be done – you can't go too much above that on the pommel horse.

It meant that knowing which routine to do became the really tough decision, and it was one that I did take Paul's advice on, at first, anyway. He'd advise me to try and qualify with an easier routine – but one that was still pretty difficult – and then pull out all the stops for the final. A lot would depend on how I felt in the final – how nervous I was and how my body felt. The years between Beijing and London would prove crucial in teaching me to listen to all those things before putting it all on the line in a big final.

I was capable of doing the most difficult routine in the world.

I still tried to stay as relaxed as I could in most of the competitions, something Paul was slowly getting used to over the years. I remember one competition – a Grand Prix in Paris – where we had a bit of time to kill before the final started. I was feeling hungry so I went to get some food, but all I could find were kebab places. I wasn't going to choose pizza and chips or a doner kebab, so I decided the healthiest option was a chicken shish kebab. It had chicken, lettuce and tomato in it, so it wasn't full of crap.

But when I got back to the warm-up gym and Paul saw what I was eating he went mad, shouting, 'What are you doing?' Twenty minutes later, though, I'd won a medal, and Paul forgot all about the kebab. If you can keep performing and winning medals, there isn't much anyone can argue with really, is there?

Heart breaker

While winning bronze in Beijing had left me trying to get used to a new life in the limelight, it had also put me in a different position when it came to major competitions. I felt under a new kind of pressure to prove that I belonged in that group of gymnasts who were considered the best in the world.

I proved it at the World Championships in 2007 and then again in Beijing, but once at the top, you have to stay there. You don't want it to look like it was just a fluke. So when I went to the European Championships in Milan, the year after Beijing, I knew I had to keep performing and keep proving myself to make sure I established my name within the gymnastics world.

As it turned out, both me and Dan Keatings did prove ourselves again in Milan. Dan won silver in the all-around competition and performed really well on the pommels, too. The final was so, so close between me, Dan and Krisztian Berki of Hungary. My first European Championships medal ended up being a silver, but I was just .05 of a mark short of Berki's gold medal winning score. And Dan was the same distance behind me.

It was a great result for GB gymnastics, and for me and Dan to be right up there with the best in the world, and I was relieved to have shown I was no fluke. But it was so very close to being an even better competition for me, and that's always frustrating.

With the pressure in the gym building to perform and achieve results, I was always looking to get involved with fun stuff outside the gym. So when I saw an advert asking for people to audition for the *X Factor* in 2009 I thought, *Why the hell not?* I've always watched it on TV and thought I'd love to do it. Especially the bit when you see all those thousands of people in the waiting room for the first auditions, all those crazy, wacky people. I thought it would be brilliant to have a go.

are you doing? There's no way you can do *X Fa*

I was just sitting on the bed watching TV when the advert inviting auditions popped up. I didn't have much on, so I filled out the form online and sent it off. When I told Paul I wanted to try out for the show he said: 'What are you doing? There's no way you can do *X Factor*. We're training for competitions. If you get through it's about three months off.'

I think he reacted that way because he thought I could go quite far in the competition. I told him that if I were to get through to a stage where there was a clash with training, I would still train, I wouldn't miss training for the *X Factor*. It was just something to do in my spare time and I wanted to see how far I could get.

The first audition I went to was at a football club in Birmingham where there were thousands and thousands and thousands of people queuing up to try out. It was cold and ridiculous – brilliant, but ridiculous. Surviving the queue is all part of the experience and I was with my mates and my brother so it was a good laugh.

I sang a song by Donnell Jones called 'U Know What's Up' and made it through to the next round of auditions, at the Birmingham NEC. They

were held indoors this time, so at least it was warmer. If you got through that, then you had to stick around for another audition, and if you made it through that second audition, then you got called back to the show.

I made it through to the fourth stage, which was the point at which you had to go up in front of Simon Cowell, Dannii Minogue and Cheryl Cole. I remember being pretty happy when Cheryl made a comment about my arms when I told them I was a gymnast, but it didn't help me get through – they gave me the boot.

I wasn't disappointed, but that day they had kept me waiting right to the end. I was the last person to go on and I didn't know the lyrics to my song that well, so I'd spent the whole day singing – trying to make sure I didn't forget the words in my audition. By the time they got to me, my throat was in bits, I needed a drink and I was so nervous. I sounded like an absolute donkey – I was rubbish. Paul was quite pleased about it, though.

So the *X Factor* fun was over, but that was probably for the best with the World Championships coming up that October. The Worlds are always important, but that year they were being held at the O2 Arena in London, where the gymnastics for the 2012 Olympics were going to be held, so it felt like an even bigger competition than normal.

At the end of August I went with the British Gymnastics squad to a training camp in Thessaloniki in Greece, to prepare for the Worlds. The idea of going abroad before a big competition is that it allows the team to get away from all the distractions of home, so we can just eat, sleep and train.

But while I was out there, I got some news that made me want to fly home as soon as possible; Nan had passed away. Paul got a phone call from my mum who was in tears, telling him what had happened and that she didn't know what to do about telling me.

Paul said that he would tell me and they'd just have to deal with whatever my reaction was. That evening, he knocked on my door and said, 'Louis, I've got some really bad news.'

I burst into tears. I completely lost it. I was shouting and banging the walls with my fists. It was devastating, and so hard to be that far away from it all. Straight away I felt I needed to be at home with my mum and brother. We're a small family and they were having to deal with it all while I was away in a different country. All I could think about was going home as soon as I possibly could.

I packed my bags and went down to reception, ready to get a cab to the airport, but Paul said they wouldn't be able to get me on a flight until the next day, and to sleep on it and we'd talk about it in the morning. It was so hard, I just wanted to go home. Eventually I listened to Paul and went back to my room, but I couldn't sleep.

All I kept thinking about was the day I'd left home for Greece. Nan had been feeling unwell and was sleeping when I was getting ready to leave, so I hadn't wanted to wake her up too much. I'd just popped my head round the door and said, 'Nan, I'm going now. I love you, see you in a bit.' So I hadn't spoken to her much at all before I went away. It was hard to grasp that I would never be able to again.

The funeral was about a week before the World Championships and it wasn't until after it was over that I was really able to think about the competition at all.

What did help during that time was that by then I was quite close to Billie, and when it was just the two of us together I felt more able to switch off and block everything out. We started to class ourselves as an official couple a week or so later, when she came to watch me at the Worlds.

I tried to use that World Championships as a way of doing something special for my nan – she was really excited about the fact I'd be competing in London, so I wanted to do well there for her. And it did start well; I qualified for the final in third place, doing my easier routine. For the final though, I decided to try out a new routine that I'd been working on in training.

I needed to start taking a step up and breaking away from what everyone else was doing because it's always about trying to stay one step ahead, and it was a good opportunity to do that.

I've done that a few times where I've gone to a competition, qualified for a final and then decided to try a newer, harder routine because that's how you start perfecting a routine – when you do it in competition, under pressure. I'd done the routine loads of times in training, but now it was time for me to put it into practice.

I was first up in the final, but only made it about halfway through my routine before I was off the pommel. The shears didn't go quite right and I think that unsettled me, so when I got to the Russians I was off balance and that was it, I came off the horse. I messed it up.

I got back on and finished my routine but I was gutted. Absolutely gutted. I sat on the floor of the arena afterwards just staring at my hands, in shock. I hate falling off, and given everything that had happened, it just made it ten times worse. I'd felt a responsibility to go through my routine, having had Nan pass away beforehand. Making a mistake didn't feel right, so it was hard. It made it a lot worse.

Normally, I'd be back on track straight away after falling in a competition. This time was different, but I've never left a competition thinking I didn't want to do the sport anymore, or wondering if I was going downhill. I've always been very motivated, so no matter what happened, if I messed up, I always left a competition thinking, *Right, let's get back in the gym and refocus.* The London Worlds was one time when I needed a few extra days to get myself back to that place mentally, though.

I sat on the floor of the arena afterwards just staring at my hands, in shock.

I don't regret competing there so soon after Nan passing away – I don't regret anything I've done. Every decision and everything I've done in the past has made me who I am. If I hadn't done that routine I might not be sitting here now with three Olympic medals. It could have changed everything.

It wasn't long after the Worlds that I decided to add to the tattoo I got after winning my first World Championship medal in 2007. 'Rest In Peace Nan, Missing You' is now forever inscribed on my back. It was my way of saying the 'goodbye' I never got to say properly in person.

At the end of that year I needed to get away for a bit, so I went to Morzine in France on a skiing holiday with Billie, one of her friends and her boyfriend. It was my first time skiing but I had one lesson on the dry slopes before we went and was pretty confident I'd pick it up quickly.

The first day on the slopes was sick. I was loving it. After about five hours of getting confident, I was coming down the slope and hit the floor hard at the bottom. It was the end of the day, just before we were going to head back to our apartment, and I'd made it all the way down before the snow turned to sheer ice and I hit a rivet or something. It was like hitting concrete.

My thumb had jammed into the ground and twisted round, but my hands were numb from being out on the snow all day so I couldn't really feel anything at first. I sat up, with my hat all wonky, and did that little check you do when you have a fall. Everything felt okay, everything was working. Legs were moving, neck was okay, upper body fine. Then I shook out my hands and something didn't feel quite right.

I took off my big glove and through the thinner glove I had on underneath I could see that my thumb was a bit bent, so I took the

Every decision and everything I've done in the past has made me who I am.

inner glove off. *Oh my God.* I've never seen anything so disgusting in my life. It was dislocated and broken – bent almost completely backwards.

I pulled it up, crunched it round and pushed it back in the socket then stuck it into the snow. Billie and the others had reached me by then and were just looking at me.

'I've fucked my thumb up,' I said, looking at Billie.

She wasn't convinced and said, 'Come on, get up, we're nearly home.'

'No, seriously. I've mashed up my thumb.'

They came a bit closer, calling me a drama queen so I pulled my thumb out of the snow. 'Oh, shit,' said Billie.

'Told ya.'

It was a nightmare. I didn't have any travel insurance because I was so used to going away with British Gymnastics who sort all that stuff out for you. I'd just gone away without thinking about it, so my thumb cost me about £600, for X-rays, plaster, more X-rays, bandaging and medication. I was lucky I had the money.

I messaged Paul when I got back to tell him what I'd done and he was livid. He was annoyed with himself too, because he had thought to tell me not to put my hands through the loops on the poles. That's more dangerous than just holding the poles, because if you fall you can't let go of them easily. And that was what had happened.

Paul thought that it would mean months of training cancelled for me and with the Europeans coming up the following April he wasn't happy. He also had the British Gymnastics guys at Lilleshall on his case asking, 'What's he doing going skiing?' But we nursed my hand through the New Year and by the end of January it was out of the cast.

All through my career, I've had people tell me not to do this because that could go wrong, or physios telling me to go easy on my wrists, but me and Paul have kind of gone against that. We've always pushed hard in training and worked around my injuries and niggles, and we've always come through. I've never really stopped training for long and I've kept on winning, so nobody really has a leg to stand on, do they?

By April, I'd proved the doubters at British Gymnastics wrong and was fit and ready to compete in the European Championships that were being held in Birmingham. We'd been hoping to finish in the top five of the team event, so when we ended up challenging for the gold it was amazing. In the end, we won silver behind Germany, but that was our best ever result in the team event at a European Championships; we'd never even won a medal before so, gold or silver, we were more than happy.

The individual finals were the following day and I had qualified on the pommel with Dan Keatings. I was first up and made a big error halfway through my routine, splitting my legs. I didn't fall off, and I finished the routine well, but I knew that mistake would probably cost me the gold if Dan or someone else went through their routine cleanly. It was made even more frustrating by the fact that the defending champion Krisztian Berki hadn't even qualified for the final.

I sat and watched the rest of the competition, mostly from behind a towel; I hate just having to wait and watch. But as the next five guys came and went, my score was still the best, no one had beaten it. Dan was second from last and coped with the pressure really well. His score was enough to push me back into second place and win him the gold, which meant a British one-two at an international competition – a huge positive for the sport in this country.

For me, it was frustrating to miss out on gold, but I think that's one of the few times Dan has beaten me on pommel in competition. If we both go clean, I think I always pip him, but I was pleased to see him win gold – I'd rather he won it than anyone else.

It was only a few days later that Dan busted his knee in training. He landed straight-legged and damaged his anterior cruciate ligament, which meant he needed a big operation and months of rehab; it was practically a year before he was back in action.

People kept asking me if I missed having him around the gym. And yeah, I missed having him there because he's a friend and we have a laugh, but in terms of training I didn't need anyone to 'bounce off'. I've never needed that. Even before I started winning, there wasn't really anyone pushing me. Some people need that, and I think I'm a good type of person for other people in the club to bounce off, but I've never really looked at someone else, been jealous of what they could do and thought that now I wanted to try.

I've always done my own thing and pushed myself and I think that's the reason I've managed to get where I am in the sport. I never waited for anyone to tell me to do this or that, and I never just went with the flow, I always pushed myself to be better.

That sometimes meant missing out on things that sounded fun but weren't necessarily the best option for my career. In 2010, that meant the Commonwealth Games in Delhi, which clashed with the World Championships in Rotterdam. The choice between the two events was a no-brainer really.

We've always pushed hard in training and worked around my injuries and niggles.

The Worlds are more important and in 2010 they were also a stepping stone towards Olympic qualification. The Commonwealth Games are great; they're a bigger spectacle and on TV but in terms of gymnastics, the World Championships are ten times more important. For my career and what it would mean in the sport, it had to be the Worlds. There really was no decision to make.

It was the first World Championships since Stuttgart in 2007 that included a team event, so it was a good chance to see how much we had improved since then, when we'd finished in 15th place. We were unbelievable in qualification, almost faultless. We ended up reaching our first World gymnastics team final in fourth place – ahead of Germany and Russia.

We knew we'd drop from that position in the final though, because of the way the scores work. In qualification, it's the best four scores that count on each piece of apparatus, but in the final, only three gymnasts get to compete on each piece, and all three scores count towards the total. That put us at a disadvantage, so we weren't expecting to maintain that 4th position.

We started the final on the pommel and I smashed my routine, scoring 15.800. After that we made a few small mistakes on the rings and floor, which held us back a bit, but we ended up in 7th place which was crazy. To come 7th in the world was amazing and the fact that we'd qualified in 4th showed the rest of the world what we were really capable of. It was a real eye-opener – for us and for everyone else.

But there was still a long way to go in terms of GB challenging for world medals, and as team captain, I made sure the boys knew that. It was like climbing Mount Everest, I told them, and we were only just out of base camp.

Qualifying for the pommel final is never easy, but in Rotterdam I put myself under so much pressure to prove that my fall in London a year earlier was a one-off. Throughout qualification for the final in Rotterdam, all I was thinking about was staying on that horse – winning never once entered my head.

If you watch that routine now, you can see my fingers digging right into the horse, I was so determined not to come off. I felt sick. I had so much to prove to Paul and everyone that I could do it. When I landed I felt like collapsing, all the hard work in the gym trying to make up for my mistake in the last World Championships had paid off.

The final turned into a story that's become a familiar one for me. My main rival, the four-time European champion Krisztian Berki, was first up and smashed his routine. He scored 15.833, which was good, but not that much higher than what I'd got in team qualifying earlier in the week.

I was sixth up and went for a 6.9 routine that was identical to the one I'd messed up at the O2 Arena in London. I wanted to show I could nail

it, and I did. It was an unbelievable routine. When I landed, I was praying it was enough for gold.

It wasn't. I was one tenth of a point away from being world champion. Berki had done an easier routine, but fair play to him, it was pretty flawless. I was asked about him by the press afterwards and I think I said something like: 'Berki is so calm and placid, he's a lot older and more experienced than me. Hopefully, I can take a leaf out of his book and settle my nerves a bit more.'

Well, I've got to compliment him at some point. And he is a fantastic competitor. He's probably messed up fewer times than I have, which is an achievement in itself, because I don't mess up very often. I wouldn't really aspire to be like anyone else though, my style is unique and I prefer it that way.

Heart breaker

127

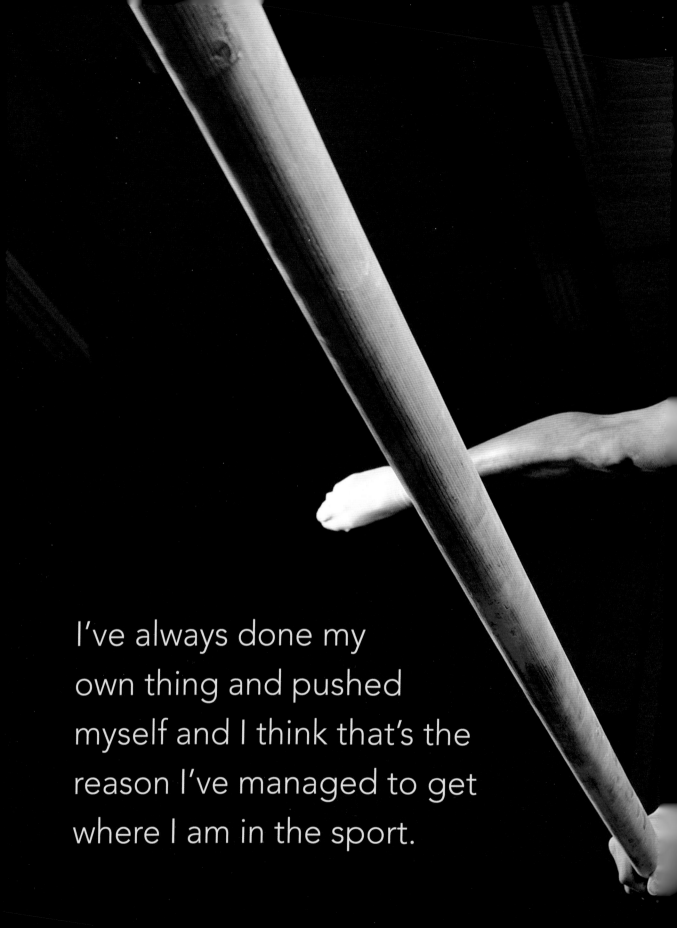

I've always done my own thing and pushed myself and I think that's the reason I've managed to get where I am in the sport.

Towards the end of the year, Gab got a phone call from adidas saying they wanted me to be in their new global TV advert for the 'All In' campaign. I'd be in it with people like David Beckham, Lionel Messi, Derrick Rose from the Chicago Bulls, Katy Perry and B.o.B. Me – Louis Smith from Peterborough – with them. Ha! It also meant flying out to Los Angeles for a few days just before Christmas, but I was pretty sure I could swing that with Paul for something so exciting.

For the advert the next day they had me pommelling on a rooftop on the outskirts of LA.

They put me and Gab in first class on a flight to New York and then from there to LA, which was unbelievable – on the second fight they had Wi-Fi on the plane. I never even knew you could get that. I was really jet lagged when we finally landed; I think I'd been away in Korea just before so my body clock was all over the place.

We went straight to a steak restaurant, which soon sorted me out. The food there was serious. It was the best steak I've ever had, and I've eaten a lot of steak. Michael Bublé was in the restaurant and Dr. Dre – it was so surreal. For the advert the next day they had me pommelling on a rooftop on the outskirts of LA, so between shots of Messi and Beckham, you can see my legs circling round a pommel – very weird.

By the time the advert aired, we were already a few months into 2011 and everything started to get a bit more real. The year before an Olympics is when everything steps up a level. Suddenly, the Games weren't just 'in 2012', they were next year. But I was in a good place having picked up silver medals at the Worlds and Europeans in 2010. Things were going well with my girlfriend Billie, too. We were still living apart – me in my flat and Billie with her mum.

With the 2011 European Championships coming up in April, I was away a lot at the start of the year, spending weeks at a time in training

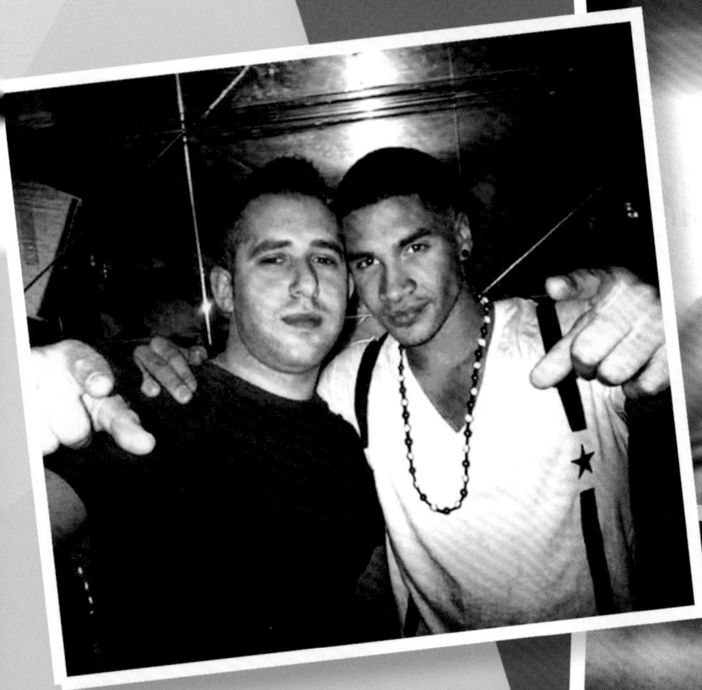

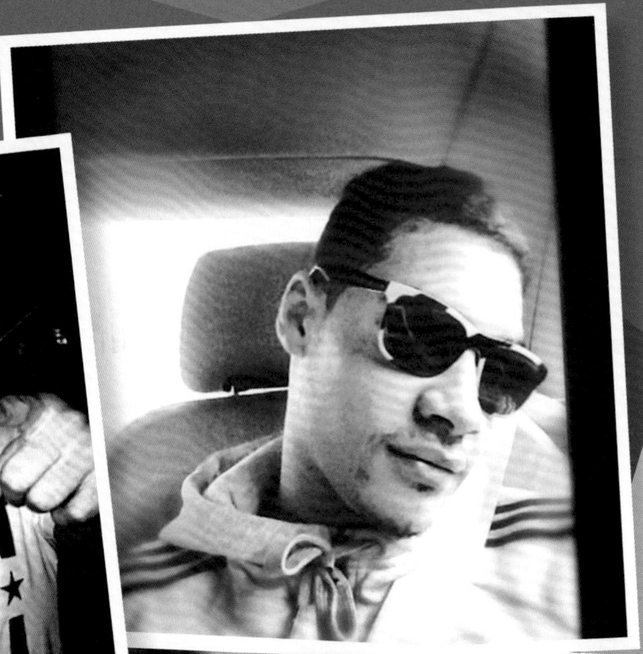

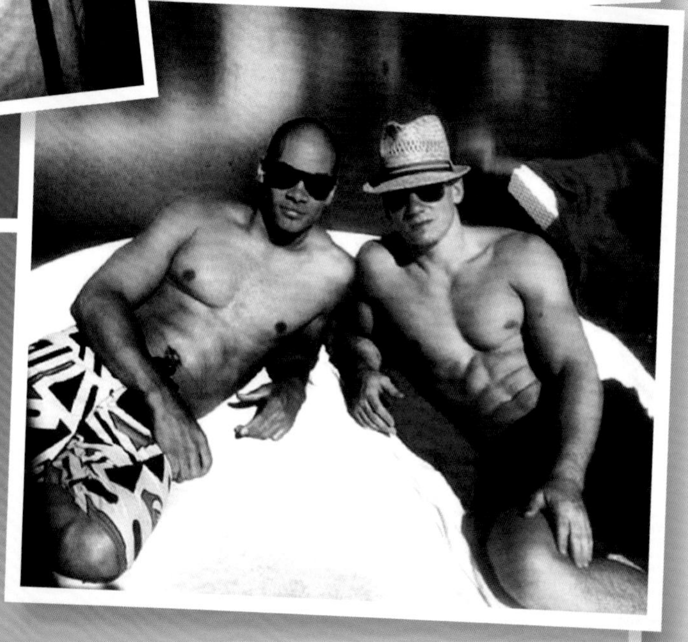

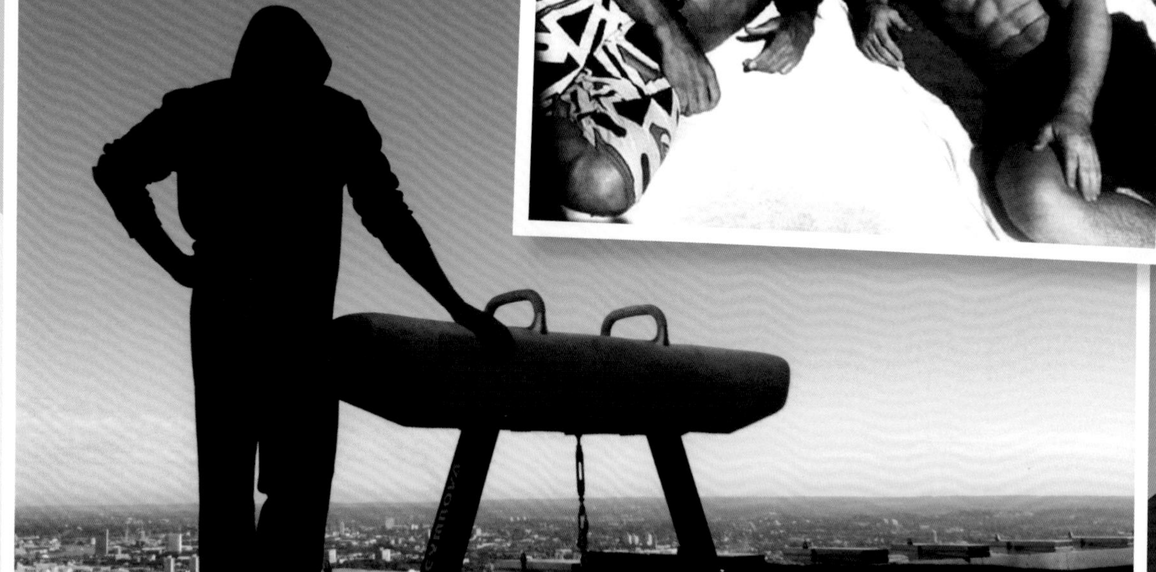

camps at the British Gymnastics base in Lilleshall. And it was around that time that Billie decided she was ready to move out of her home and we should start looking for a place together. She'd ring me, asking if we should do this or that. But I had no time to think about helping her to find a new place while I was trying to focus on getting ready for the European Championships. It was the wrong time but she couldn't seem to see that, she was just set on the idea of moving out as soon as she could.

I went to Berlin with the team for the Europeans and tried to dismiss all the stuff going on at home. I wasn't stressing about it or making any big decisions, I'd just speak to Billie on the phone and say 'Yeah, cool, whatever' any time she brought it up.

The Europeans was a competition I felt ready for; I was fit and mentally I felt like I was in the right place. So when I qualified for the final with no problems, I knew that as long as I went through my routine cleanly, I should be leaving with a medal.

But just as I was getting into my routine, at the point when I'm about to start the Russian – the hard part – one of those big camera booms goes right underneath me, in the opposite direction to the way I'm circling. I spot it, look at it, and that split second is enough – I'm off the pommel.

I was so pissed off. I hadn't even needed a lot to win. Normally, if I make a mistake in competition it's like, *Okay, it's a bit annoying, let's get back on, finish off, it doesn't really matter.* But because I'd made a mistake and it wasn't my fault, it really, *really* pissed me off. It got under my skin. It's one thing for me to make an error, but for someone else to have caused it – as I said, I was pissed off.

I didn't really know what to do. I didn't know I could have complained about it straight away because it had never happened before, to anyone. I just kept my mouth shut and got back on to finish my routine. I didn't really want to bring it up immediately in the mixed zone afterwards, because I didn't want it to look like I was making excuses, even though the only reason I fell off was that camera.

So what was I supposed to say in the interviews? I just said, 'There was a bit of confusion with the cameras and stuff but ultimately, it's my fault.' Afterwards we put in an official complaint and the organisers looked back at the footage. They saw the camera coming in front of me and said that if I had complained right away, I could have had another go. Great, cheers.

I was still fucked off when I got back from Berlin. So when I was greeted by Billie and this completely new house that I'd seen just once before, and that now had all my stuff from my old place in it, I was like *What?* I was stressed after everything that had gone on at the Euros and we ended up having an argument that ended with me leaving, saying, 'I think we should have a bit of a break.'

I moved back in with Mum for a bit and things went downhill between me and Billie from there – they got really sour. I didn't want to keep living at Mum's; I'd gone from being independent to living under her roof again and I missed having my own space, so eventually it meant Billie moving out of the flat.

Billie thought that was it, that we were finished. But after a few weeks, once I'd pieced myself back together, relaxed and got over everything I rang her up to try and talk and see if we could sort things out. She said, 'Louis, I'm going to Ibiza for six months.' What could I do? She'd already booked the trip and decided she was going.

It destroyed me. Completely disengaging from Billie had made me realise how much I loved her and wanted to be with her. That was the whole idea of having a break. So when she went out to Ibiza, my world was just crushed, I couldn't do anything. I was supposed to be going to an international competition in Moscow about a week later – a trip Paul had spent ages organising, sorting out visas and other stuff. I sent him a text the day before we were due to fly, simply saying: 'Paul, can't go to Moscow tomorrow. Sorry x.'

I was stressed after everything that had gone on at the Euros and we ended up having an argument that ended with me leaving.

He tried to call me but I wasn't up to talking to anyone, I just wanted to be left alone. I tried to train but I felt completely lost in the gym. I drove to one session and couldn't even get out of the car to go in – I just sat in the car park for an hour and then drove home. I couldn't eat or sleep properly either. If I wasn't crying, I'd be up all night just thinking, 'What's she doing? Who's she with?'

I wrote some song lyrics about how I felt as I thought it might help me to get the emotions out and maybe even get Billie's attention. Singing helped too, so I recorded them and posted the song on YouTube, hoping I'd get a reaction from her. I did get one. She didn't like it. She rang me up shouting, 'I can't believe you'd do that . . . all my friends have seen it.'

I didn't want to talk to anyone about how I felt, because as soon as I did, I'd start getting upset again. And my friends would only say stuff like, 'Just get over it, it's fine. Everyone has break-ups. I remember when I split up with . . .'

'No, it's different,' I'd try to tell them. When I got together with Billie it had been at a tough time in my life, after Beijing and then with Nan passing away, and she'd helped me get through it. Just being with her had made things better, so it wasn't like a normal relationship; she was kind of my saving grace. So it meant a lot more than a normal break-up.

It was a scary time in my life, I was so messed up. I just tried to disengage from everything. It killed me. Now, I'm no alcoholic and I've never agreed with the idea of turning to drink to avoid any problems in your life, but i'll admit that at the time, I'd even have some wine now and again to send me off to sleep.

Normally, I wear my heart on my sleeve and if I'm going to get involved with someone, I'll go for it.

Gradually, I guess your body finds ways of mending itself. You put up barriers and walls to try and help you get through. But even now I still feel like I'd never be able to let myself go in a relationship, because I'd be scared that if anything went wrong, I'd be how I was then. That whole scenario scares me – that pain. If you don't let yourself get like that again with someone, then you won't feel that pain again.

It's not the right way to be and it's why I've not been in a proper relationship with anyone since then, because it would be unfair to them. Normally, I wear my heart on my sleeve and if I'm going to get involved with someone, I'll go for it. But if I was to do that now it would end up not working – I know it. So I guess I just have to wait for that fear to go away.

I had two big guardian angels tattooed on my back not long after me and Billie split up when I felt I could manage and was back on track. I had them to represent the fact that I had two guardian angels to help me get through the bad times. They didn't hurt as much as my first tattoo, but they were still pretty sore – they go right over the muscles on my back.

The angels are actually a work in progress. I still want to add the pearly gates between the angels' hands, the steps up to heaven and some clouding and shading. Heaven is bliss, it's peaceful and I believe if you do things right and take the right path in life, that's where you'll end up. So I obviously did listen to some things at Sunday school.

7

Testing times

It was months after my break-up with Billie before things began to feel any easier. It probably wasn't until just before the World Championships in Tokyo, later that year, that I actually started to feel capable of doing the job I needed to do. It still didn't feel right though – not really. It was as though I'd been in a war and my leg had been blown open and a mate had said, 'Let's just quickly sew it up, that'll hold for now.' It felt like that – I'd just been patched up for the moment.

Tokyo was where we were planning to qualify the GB teams for London 2012, and after the Worlds in Rotterdam a year earlier, where we'd qualified for the team final in fourth place, the mood was positive. We were going to Tokyo to try and make sure GB had a full men's team at the Olympics for the first time since Barcelona in 1992.

I was very sure of my job and what I needed to do (Kristian Thomas was the team captain in Tokyo) and the guys were sure of theirs, but there was this expectation from having done so well the year before. The coaches were thinking that it was our chance to be right up there before the Olympic Games and maybe even sneak a medal.

The effect of that on the boys is hard to explain – I've been in that position before, where you have the burden of expectation. I had it at the Worlds in 2009, when I really felt I needed to win that competition, but instead I completely messed it up. So I'd learnt not to go into a competition thinking that I needed to do this or that. I learnt to just go there and enjoy it. But Tokyo was the first time there was a real sense of expectation and the boys felt it – they just didn't know how to deal with it. And it broke us down.

The breaking point came on the high bar, when Ruslan Panteleymonov (who moved to Britain from Ukraine to study in 2000 and became a British citizen in 2008) fell during his routine and then Dan Keatings did the same. He fell really badly, crashing flat on his back and whacking his head. From then on the mistakes kept on coming, and from pretty much every direction. It was really only Dan Purvis and me who managed to

I'd done everything I could for the team up to that moment, but then it was my time.

ignore all the carnage; Dan did well enough to qualify for the all-around final and I scored 15.600 on the pommel which qualified me for the final. But for the team, it wasn't enough. We finished in 10th place, two places below what we needed to qualify for the Olympics.

I had to put the disappointment to one side and concentrate on getting ready for the pommel final a few days later. I'm a team player and I'll do everything I can to help the team, but, as selfish as it sounds, as soon as it's time for the pommel horse in a competition, it's just me. That is my job, it's my livelihood, it's who I am. Everything is about that moment, so I have to be selfish.

I'd done everything I could for the team up to that moment, but then it was my time to zone out and think about myself. I was going for a 7.1-value routine in the final – the hardest I'd ever gone for in competition – but I messed it up. It was also the first time I'd gone for that routine

in a competition and I didn't really know how to prepare for it. So in the warm-up gym I did routine after routine after routine, panicking that I hadn't done enough. In the end, I actually did too much. When it came to the final, I was knackered.

I went second out of the eight finalists. I made it through most of my routine but I messed up the dismount at the end. By then, my arms were all over the place. I had nothing left in them; they were like jelly. Although my score of 15.066 took the lead, with six other gymnasts to go including Krisztian Berki, my other close rivals Cyril Tommasone from France and Prashanth Sellathurai from Australia, the best all-around gymnast in the world Kohei Uchimura and the 2004 Olympic Pommel Horse Gold Medalist Teng Haibin still to go, it would take an absolute miracle to stay in the medal positions.

Cyril went straight after me and went clean, pushing me down into the silver medal position already. Then, out of nowhere, Uchimura, who was having the Championships of his life, messed up. The whole place was shocked. Next up, Prashanth. He messed up. It was already too much for me to take, and I think from then on I had my jacket over my head. Berki went second last and nailed his routine. The gold medal was all but his and I was now in bronze medal position with the former Olympic Champion to go. All he needed to do was beat what was a fairly average score on my part due to the deductions for my dismount.

I told Mum off afterwards because she said she prayed to Nan for a miracle to happen on that day, and it did. Teng Haibin seemed to be cruising to a medal, pushing me off the podium, then somehow his legs just stuck on the pommel on one of his rotations and he was off. I couldn't believe it. I'd won the bronze medal, which might have looked like a step back after I'd won silver in Rotterdam, but I left Tokyo happy with my performance.

Before I competed I'd spoken to Paul and said, 'Look, if I'm going to do this routine at the Olympics I need to try and do it now.' He agreed. I just needed to go for it and keep doing the routine in that kind of pressured situation. So I'd known there was a high chance I wasn't going to do well in Tokyo and that I could fall off or mess up. We'd been in this situation before – at the Worlds in 2009 – where I'd also tried a new routine, so we knew it could backfire. But it's hard to replicate the pressures of competition in training, so we decided it was best to do it at an event like Tokyo.

I went for it and pretty much got to the end; I'd done the hard part before I fell off. So it was a confidence boost more than a disappointment. I'd done the hardest routine in the world in a pressurised situation and got all the hard stuff right.

I'd done the hardest routine in the world in a pressurised situation.

As far as the team performance went, I didn't really feel like I could have helped the boys any more to prepare for the expectations people had of them. Everyone's different, so my way might not have been right for them. They needed to understand for themselves what they had to do to get into the zone. While I can see now that it was a good experience for them to have before London, we could have done with it two years earlier.

It made everything a bit scary, because to qualify for the Olympics as an individual, you had to win a medal at the Worlds – which I did – but you also had to compete on two other pieces of apparatus – which I didn't. So the only way for me to get to the Games was for the team to qualify, which we had assumed they would do in Tokyo.

Instead, everything was resting on one last chance of qualification, at the Olympic Test Event in London the following January. That's where we'd be fighting against all the other teams that had finished between 9th and 16th places in Tokyo for the last four team slots at the Games. I was fairly confident that as long as we didn't have a blowout, we'd finish in the top four, but everyone knew what was at stake if we didn't. It would mean only one male gymnast would get to compete for Team GB at the Games six months later, and there were no guarantees who that gymnast would be.

That Christmas was a quiet one. We had three or four days off and then two days at New Year before it was straight back into some intense training. It was full on right from the start – there was no piddling about as there usually is after the Christmas break – but everyone was prepared to do that because it was about qualifying for the Olympics.

It wasn't an easy time but we tried to turn it into something positive. The Test Event was being held at the Olympic venue – the O2 Arena – so competing in it would give us a chance to get used to the surroundings before our main rivals, who had already qualified in Tokyo. We'd be able to try out the equipment and the format they were going to use for the Games. All those factors helped to put us back in the right frame of mind whenever we started to get down about training through Christmas.

Our first piece was the high bar – it had to be, after what happened in Tokyo. I could see there were some nerves twitching among the boys beforehand, so I told them to chill, to see it as just a bigger national championships. It seemed to do the trick and we went into the second rotation in 5th place before moving up to 4th after the floor.

The pommel was next and I decided to play it relatively safe, knowing a solid score was needed to settle us into the top four. I punched the air after I landed my routine clean and with Max Whitlock and Dan Keatings also scoring highly, it meant we moved up into first place. And that was where we finished, with a performance good enough to have put us in fifth place in Tokyo. That didn't matter though. All that mattered was we had secured our place at London 2012 and shown that if we hit our routines, we could hold our own with the best in the world.

But what sticks in my head most from the Test Event, is that I was overweight. I might have performed well, but I was two to three kilos above what I should have been. It might not sound like much, but trust

me, when you're balancing on your wrists for 50 seconds at a time, it's definitely too much.

A comfortable weight for me is about 78kg but I was about 82kg for the Test Event. Then we went to Mexico for a training camp and my weight went up. British Gymnastics didn't want us to go on holiday with the Games only six months away, so they took us to Mexico for a sort of working holiday. It was warm, and we were in an all-inclusive holiday resort where we drank and ate lots. I said to them at the time it was a stupid idea, and I should just stay at home and relax but they didn't listen.

By the time we got back home my weight had increased again and had to tell Paul I was 85.5kg.

'What? You'll never be able to lose that for the Olympics. That's it, there's just no way you're going to be able to lose eight kilos in time for the Games.'

He was so negative about it but I was pretty confident I could prove him wrong. I changed my diet, trained properly, started running and gradually my weight started to come down. I'd go into training every couple of weeks and say 'I'm down to 84kg, Paul,' then 82kg . . . .

By the time it was the Games I was 77kg and I was happy with that, it was perfect. I was in such good shape, primed and ready to go. And Paul never said another word about it.

Losing the weight was made a bit easier by the fact that when we got back from Mexico, training got more intense. We'd qualified for the Games but that still meant we only had five places but around thirteen boys who wanted them, so everyone started trying to prove themselves. Everyone rushed to get to as many international competitions as possible to try and get the scores that would help prove they should be picked.

In April, I had a World Cup Series event to go to in Zibo, China. It was just going to be me and Paul there and I didn't really want to go. But, as it turned out, about ten days before the trip it looked like I might not be able to go anyway. I was training on the high bar and missed my catch after a double back somersault, stubbing my finger so hard on the bar that I fractured it. It was horrible. My friend Luke was holding the crash pad and when I hit the bar and landed in the pit, he just went, 'Urggghhhh, I heard that crack.'

Gymnasts are no strangers to a bit of pain.

What he heard was the bone snapping. At hospital they taped it up; it was my ring finger so they strapped it against my middle one and said it would take around a month to heal. *Shit*. It suddenly hit me. This thing in China was selection stuff and I needed to prove I was fit when they made the selection. Now I'd hurt my finger a week before I was to go to one of my selection competitions.

'Can I still compete?' I asked the doctor. Everyone at the hospital advised me not to, but I'd already decided; it would be fine. I had a photo shoot to do the day after I had it strapped up and the press went nuts about it; it was in all the papers and on TV. It wasn't even a story, really. In the end we had to put out a statement saying it wasn't as bad as first thought and I was still able to train and hopefully compete in China.

Training was painful and I had to change the way I held the handle of the pommel slightly to avoid putting too much pressure on it, but I gritted my teeth and got on with it. I was just relieved I wasn't going to have to sit and watch everyone else training for a month.

People were making such a big deal out of my injury, but gymnasts are no strangers to a bit of pain – we get strapped up and get on with the job, no harm done. So, with a broken finger, jet lag and feeling ill after I'd picked up a bug on the plane, I came second in China, winning silver just behind Krisztian Berki. I did a new routine in the final, too – one of my harder routines with the Russians – and was only 0.150 points off gold in the end.

It was a good result, but I still had more competitions to do to prove I was ready, and we wanted to compete with the new routine as much as possible. For most of 2012, I'd qualify for the finals of competitions with my easy routine then bring out the harder one in the final – it just meant adding one, two or three Russians, depending on how hard I wanted to make it.

My finger making the news rammed home for me how crazy the media interest was, and I knew it was only going to get worse. There were interviews to do, sponsor events to go to. It seemed like every day there was a list of stuff to get through. It was hard to try and find slots for interviews that didn't interfere with training, especially as I was in Lilleshall with the team for a lot of the time.

Did I ever think it was too much? All the time. When you're training six days a week for thirty-two hours a week, a lot of the time you just want a few hours to breathe – time to relax. But I suppose that's all part of being a top athlete, you just have to push through it. I'd had quite a bit of media interest before and after Beijing so I knew it was going to be hard and there'd be increased expectation, but knowing it's going to be hard and actually dealing with it are two different things.

I was wary of going out and having a drink, because I wanted to eliminate any risk of something going wrong. I just liked to do nothing.

My phone did my head in – I couldn't stand my phone. It must have been so annoying for my friends to message me and not get anything back, but I just wanted to chill out when I wasn't training.

There were some bits of the media that I enjoyed doing, though; like the Team GB kit launch. It was a chance to show off the kit that British athletes would be wearing at the Games, which had all been designed by Stella McCartney.

I travelled down to London the night before the launch and met up with Carmen, who works for adidas, to talk through what they wanted me to do in the show. She said I'd be hoisted up in the air doing bits and pieces with a pommel. I just nodded, 'Yeah, yeah, sounds great,' but didn't really take in what she was saying.

We did a few dress rehearsals the next day but they wanted me to do my pommel horse routine in mid-air, after I'd been hoisted some 20 feet up. It would have looked good, but it also would have been really dangerous so we quickly said, 'Er, no.' Plan B was to have me balancing on a pommel horse that was raised up out of this huge box on the stage, so it still looked cool.

Stella wasn't there for rehearsals, but we met her just before the actual show and she was really lovely – she knew who everyone was and what we all did. There were so many athletes and Paralympians there – all in the same room backstage – that it felt like the Olympics had arrived already and I was about to walk out into the Olympic Stadium. It was quite surreal. I'd tried the kit on before for photo shoots, but there had been a lot of secrecy over the design, so we'd never been allowed to take it away from the shoots. It was nice to finally get to show it off.

We did loads and loads and loads of media after the show, but all I really remember is that I got pooed on. I was doing an interview outside and was standing underneath a tree in my leotard when a bird pooed on my shoulder. It ricocheted off my bare skin and landed on the interviewer's leg, dribbling all over his jeans. I just had a little smudge, which came off with a wet wipe, but his jeans were covered in it.

While I'd been doing that, I'd missed the stuff kicking off about the kit being too blue. Then I looked on Twitter and saw everyone moaning about it – there's not enough red, it's too blue. Blue, blue, blue, blah, blah, blah. It was stupid. At a kit launch, you really want everyone to look like they're part of the same team, which means everyone should be wearing a uniform that links them together. So what would be the point in a kit launch where one athlete is in blue, then one in red, then blue again? We would have looked mismatched if they had done that. The whole idea was to have everyone dressed in the same design, but that didn't mean there couldn't be any red kit. For the gymnastics squad there were three types of leotard – a dark blue one, a light blue and a red one – but for the launch they wanted me in the blue one.

My next appearance that day was on Channel 4 News, where I was appearing with the Paralympic sprinter Stefanie Reid. We were being interviewed about the kit by Jon Snow, so I said to the girl from adidas, 'Let me put the red kit on.' I had my tracksuit on over the top of the leotard, but I really wanted to wear the red one to shut everyone up about the blue. They said, 'Oh, just take your jacket off to show it,' but I thought, *No, I'm going to show them how red this thing is.*

A few minutes into the interview, Jon Snow asked me about the kit. 'Where's the red, it is a blue thing isn't it?'

So I took off my jacket and said, 'I'm wearing the red leotard, I'll give you a little twirl. I've done two naked photo shoots, so posing in a leotard is fun.'

He seemed a bit surprised and sort of stumbled, 'Well that is some body, I mean, let alone the er, let alone the shirt . . .'

I carried on, taking off my tracksuit bottoms to show the bottom half of the leotard.

'Oh, how far are you going? I see. Terrific.'

'I'll keep going 'til you want me to stop,' I joked.

'Ha ha no, well once you've got, er, I think that, that might be far enough. That is quite fantastic. That's . . . that's nice, isn't it?'

I carried on, explaining that what they were trying to do with the launch was show Team GB is a unit, and that behind the scenes there was a whole red range that wasn't being seen. He was still stumbling . . .

It was just my way of saying, 'Shut up and stop moaning.'

'If you don't mind me saying, that is pectorally uplifting.'

'No, that's just all muscle,' I replied.

By this point, Gab says everyone watching in the green room was pissing themselves laughing but I had no idea it was that funny until I saw Jon Snow was trending on Twitter and watched it to see why. I was just trying to show everyone the whole shebang – maybe I should've warned him first.

On my way back to Peterborough I decided to tweet my thoughts on the kit, just in case anyone had missed them. I wrote, 'Finally on my way home after an eventful day, GB kit is sick. #hushyourgums.'

Adidas liked the hash tag so much they used it in one of their adverts before the Games – it was just my way of saying, 'Shut up and stop moaning.' Hush your gums, basically.

A few months later it was the European Championships, our last major international competition before the Games. It was exciting, being at an event like that with the Olympics just three months away, and the fact that we nailed it showed us that we were almost ready.

We'd qualified for the final of the team event in first place, but we knew the Russians, Germans and the French, who were hosting the event, would step up in the final. And Russia did lead for most of the competition. I'd scored the highest mark of the day on the pommel, though, and Ruslan Panteleymonov nailed a massive vault, just as one of the Russians fell off the high bar.

Suddenly, we were leading the competition; the French were having a nightmare and the Germans were struggling too. Our last piece was the high bar and I knew that if Max Whitlock and Kristian Thomas nailed their routines, we'd win gold. But Max fell off on his Markelov. I saw him walk away with an 'Oh my God, I can't believe I've just done that' look on his face.

It came down to Kristian, who was the last gymnast to perform, so the whole arena was watching him. The whole place was dead quiet and the risk factor in his routine was serious. We knew he needed to score at least 14.372 for us to win gold, but he was solid as a rock, going clean and scoring 15.133. It was unbelievable.

We rewrote the record books with that result – it was Britain's first ever European team gold and in terms of preparing for the Olympics, we couldn't have asked for a more positive result. It had only been seven months since we'd finished 10th in Tokyo but it felt like we were a completely different team. A team that believed in itself.

In the pommel final a day later, it was me against Berki for the gold, again. I went through my routine clean and got a good score, but then Berki scored higher than me on execution. Paul noticed right away that Berki's start value was wrong – they'd given him a 6.9, the same as me, but his routine had missed one of the rotations needed to make it a 6.9.

I'd gone out to get a crêpe after I'd finished competing. There was a stall selling them in the arena and it was the treat all the gymnasts allowed themselves once they'd finished. When I got back, Paul was still talking to one of the judges. Then one judge turned to me and said that they'd messed up and I should be European champion. I couldn't really

say anything to that. I wasn't going to kick off there and then, so I just accepted my silver medal and tried to smile for the podium pictures.

But it did piss me off. It could have been my last European Championships and I should have won gold. Paul told me that the head judge sent a letter to British Gymnastics afterwards, apologising for getting it wrong, which was something, but I'd have preferred the medal.

One judge turned to me and said that they'd messed up and I should be European champion.

I knew then that the Olympic gold would probably come down to another battle between me and Berki. If one of us made a mistake then others would come into it, but otherwise there were two levels of pommel specialists: me and Berki, a Chinese guy who didn't get selected in the end, and the Australian, Prashanth Sellathurai, who didn't qualify, were all one one level; then there was everyone else – people like Max Whitlock and Robert Seligman, who were there or thereabouts. But if both Berki and I went through to the final, I knew it would be between him and me.

It might sound weird, but I'm pleased Berki has been around during my career. If not, it would have been boring. Don't get me wrong, it would have been amazing if he hadn't been in the sport – I'd love to have been world champion for the last four years in a row, but it's good to have someone to make it interesting. Otherwise, if people know you're just going to keep winning it takes the edge off things a bit.

At the British Championships in Liverpool the month after the Europeans, there was no Berki, just British gymnasts trying to prove their form and fitness before the Olympic squads were officially announced at the beginning of July. It was so intense. I had never assumed that just because I'd won a medal in Beijing I'd be in the squad, because the team had come on so much since 2008. There was so much more competition for places than there had been before.

I got a huge score on the pommel that day – 16.375 points – so I knew I'd done everything I could to make the team. When the final announcement came it was such a relief, but it was hard to see others miss out. I'd trained with Dan Keatings for so many years, so when he didn't make the cut it was hard. He'd looked fit and ready, so it was tough not to see him get picked. Having to watch how well everyone did at the Games, and knowing that you had the potential to be in that team and do just as well must have been so frustrating. I really feel for him. I'd love to see him go on to compete in Rio in 2016.

Once the teams had been finalised, it was only a week or so before I was packing my bag for the Olympic preparation camp. I've been to countless preparation camps ahead of big competitions over the years, but this one was different. It was July and there were just three weeks to go before our first day of competition at the 2012 Olympic Games.

Why was it so different? Mostly because this time I actually saw the sense in being there. In earlier years, going away to train had always just felt a bit irrelevant. I never understood why being somewhere else – somewhere strange and new – was any better than training at home, going back to my own comfy sofa at the end of the day and being able to sleep in my own bed.

But this time, I got it. It felt so good to get away and leave behind the constant interviews, daily scare stories about overcrowded tubes and tempting invitations to go out with friends. Going to France before the Games meant that all distractions were removed and all we had to do was train, eat, sleep and then repeat the whole cycle, day after day after day. This time, I could see that with the biggest competition of my life looming, it was the only way to prepare properly.

So I left for two weeks in Arques, just across the Channel, feeling relieved at having escaped the madness. That feeling didn't last too long once we got there, though. Training in that first week was balls to the wall kind of stuff; really intense. We'd do routine after routine after routine. In one morning session alone, we might do two floor routines,

two on pommels, one on rings, three vaults, two on parallel bars and two on high bars. The second session of the day would then include repeat parts and half routines – it was a 'get in the hours' type of week. And it was incredibly tough.

The following week was about tapering down rather than ramping things up. The first half was about doing one or two clean routines. If you did your first routine with no mistakes, you were allowed to move on to the next one, but if you messed up, then you'd have to do it again. The second half of the week was more to do with competition practice. So you'd do a routine, then put your hand up and get your scores from the coaches, just as if you were at the Games.

It was serious stuff, but I tried to take the edge off it with some fun and games when I got the chance. It's always good to have someone around the team who can walk into a room and chill everyone out a bit, especially ahead of an Olympic Games, when the intensity can build up to a crazy level if you let it. I played tricks on people like I've always done and answered the coaches back, but one thing I've learned over the years is to make sure I choose the right time to do it; the mood has to be right.

I know now that it's not only the gymnasts who get stressed – the coaches do too. My coach, Paul is always quite chilled and at London 2012 he already had the experience of Beijing behind him, but some of the coaches hadn't been to an Olympics for a while. They were all so determined to get the best out of everyone for those two weeks in Arques and I could see that they were getting quite uptight.

It probably didn't help that we were training in the same gym as the teams from France and Japan. The coaches have so much pride in their team and you could tell that they all wanted to show off what their gymnasts could do in front of the other teams. Whenever one of us landed a clean routine, you could see them look around to check if anyone else had caught a glimpse of it. But if we made a mistake, you'd see them getting quite frustrated.

The coaches might have been keeping an eye on the two teams we'd be competing against in a few weeks' time, but for the gymnasts, it wasn't really like that. We'd chat quite happily to the French guys, get our training done and leave. We didn't sit there making notes or take secret videos on our phones, or anything like that.

If you're worried about getting new injuries or accidentally hurting yourself, then you won't be attacking your routines like you need to.

We were quite in awe of the Japanese gymnasts, though. They won the Olympic team silver medal in Beijing and are one of the best teams in the world. We aspire to be like them one day. At the moment I don't think we're anywhere near them, although as we saw at the Games, anyone can make a mistake in gymnastics.

I'm always carrying little aches and pains in my body, but I was pleased with how I felt in France. It can be difficult, when it gets so close to a big competition, to balance training hard enough with staying fit and healthy, but in gymnastics you can't wrap yourself up in cotton wool. If you're worried about getting new injuries or accidentally hurting yourself, then you won't be attacking your routines like you need to. In a sport like gymnastics you just have to go for it, which can be quite scary when there's something as big as a home Olympics around the corner.

In my own mind, I knew my capabilities, and although London 2012 was big – well, massive – I had to treat it just like any other competition. I've only ever once gone into a competition expecting to walk away with a medal, and it didn't work at all, so it's something I've never done since. I was just planning to go to London and concentrate on doing my routine as well as I could. I had spent the years leading up to 2012 trying to tell the other boys in the team to take the same approach and as time went on I started hearing it in their interviews, 'We just want to go there and focus on what we have to do.' So I knew it was sinking in.

If you repeat those kinds of things enough times, you put less pressure on yourself, something that we already had more than enough of. In the last few years we've been doing well in gymnastics and people were starting to recognise us as a nation that finishes in the top handful at competitions, one that's capable of winning medals. But if we had started to think that we needed to perform this time or people would be disappointed, it would have resulted in extra pressure that we really didn't need. So I didn't want any talk of medals, of any colour, in France. At the back of my mind I always knew that if my routine went well then I could get a medal, but I had to try and ignore that.

There were just four days to go before the start of the Games when we left France for a London that was waiting to see what the Olympics would bring. On our last night at the camp we had been told to be ready to leave for 11.15 a.m., so we woke up in good time, ate breakfast and went back to our rooms to get the washing in and get packed up. About an hour before our coach was due to leave there was a knock at my door. It was the drug testers doing one of their random out of competition checks.

It wouldn't have been a problem if I hadn't gone to the toilet about 20 minutes earlier. As it was, I had a massive dilemma: I couldn't pee and the coach was due to leave shortly to take us to the rail station. It was a nightmare. The British coaches were ringing up the anti-doping people asking if I had to do the test there and then, or if we could drive to somewhere else and do it before we got on the train.

In the end the bus left without me, and one of the coaches, Eddie. We didn't have a car so we began trying to convince the drug tester to drive us to the train station, which isn't really allowed. Luckily, about 10 minutes after the coach left I managed to produce enough fluid to satisfy the testers. Eddie called the others straight away and they got the coach to come back for us – I'd pissed just in time. It was very nearly a disaster.

I couldn't believe it when we arrived in London a few hours after that episode, to see the rainy city we had left behind a few weeks ago was now soaked in sunshine. It felt good. It felt exciting. And I felt ready.

Almost perfect

Arriving at the Olympic Village about three days before the opening ceremony, it felt like the whole world was there. We queued up in a huge check-in area – a bit like the ones at the airport with body and bag scanners – to get security checked and registered before we could get in, alongside hundreds of other sportspeople. The only thing that we had in common was that every single athlete was buried beneath a massive pile of kit.

The whole of Team GB was housed in two big blocks of flats; we had the cyclists and hockey teams in our block, but on our floor it was just gymnastics people. The men's and women's squads, the coaches, directors, team managers, doctors and physios were all conveniently (or annoyingly) nearby.

Me, Sam Oldham, Kristian Thomas, Dan Purvis and Max Whitlock were in one big apartment that had three bedrooms, a living room and a little balcony overlooking the Olympic Park. One of those bedrooms was just for me, which was a relief as I'd been a bit worried about having to share for the whole Olympics. It's not that I don't get on with the other boys, but having moved out of home when I was 19, I'm used to having my own space and I like my privacy. As it turned out, I was in one room, with Dan and Kristian and then Max and Sam in the others. Most importantly, the team PlayStation was a firm fixture in the living room.

Once we were settled in and I had arranged my room as I wanted it, I went into Kristian's room and found him struggling to sort out his air conditioning unit. They were big machines with a pipe coming out of the

I knew I had a job to do, so I chilled out, got the job done and enjoyed looking around afterwards.

back that you're supposed to leave poking out of the window because it pumps out all the warm air.

'I'll sort it out for you, Kris,' I said, casually hiding the pipe round the back of his curtain while he was busy unpacking. 'All sorted,' I smiled, before heading back to my own, pleasantly cool room.

A few hours later, Kristian started complaining that it was even more roasting in his room than before. For the whole evening he was up and down, up and down, and his T-shirt was developing more sweat patches by the minute. When he was about to go to bed I thought, *I can't let him sleep like that*, so I went into his room which by then was like a sauna, and chucked the pipe out of the window. It was pretty funny, although I was definitely laughing about it more than Kristian.

Out of all our team at the Games, Kristian was the closest to me in age; he's just a couple of months older than me. while Dan is two years younger than me. Sam and Max were the two youngest in the team. I've competed in teams with Kristian and Dan for quite a few years now and trained with Sam at Huntingdon for the past five years so I know him really well – it was a really cool team.

Once we got into the Village, though, it soon became clear that one of us needed reigning in a bit. Max was so easily excitable, we'd be sitting

in the apartment and I would casually mention I was just going to nip out to get a drink. That was enough to set him off. 'I'll come, I'll come!' He had his shoes on and was out of the door almost before I had finished my sentence.

When I went to Beijing I remember how tempting it was to walk around the Village exploring and going to the hospitality zone all the time, but even back then no one had to tell me to tone it down. I knew I had a job to do, so I chilled out, got the job done and enjoyed looking around afterwards. Four years on, I was the only one with Olympic experience in the team and was the team captain, so I felt it was my job to set an example for the way the others behaved around the Village. With someone who is quite excitable like Max, it was up to people like me and Kristian, who's a really calm kind of guy, to keep an eye on him and make sure he stayed as chilled out as possible.

So it was probably a good thing that a few days after our arrival in the Village we had to watch the Olympic opening ceremony from our balcony.

The men's team qualifying event was the next morning so there was zero chance of us being allowed to march into the stadium with the rest of Team GB. It would have meant spending hours on our feet and getting just a few hours' sleep, neither of which is ideal preparation for a big competition.

It's always the same; in Beijing we were competing the day after the opening ceremony and at the Commonwealth Games in Melbourne, too, so I've never actually been to an Olympics opening. Maybe I'll finally get the chance to attend one at the Rio Games in 2016 – although it may well have to be as a spectator. But if I'm competing, then it'll no doubt be the same story all over again.

We were watching the opening ceremony on TV until we saw the Queen hovering over the Park in a helicopter. We jumped up and ran to the balcony for a better view of her – well, someone dressed as her – skydiving into the stadium, it was brilliant. I had always wondered what they might do for an opening ceremony in Britain and this was really cool. It showed how different we are from everyone else, something I always see as a good thing. Who wants to be the same as everyone else?

Not long after that I went to bed, pretty sure it wasn't going to get any better than the Queen skydiving with James Bond, but I just lay there wide awake, staring at the ceiling for hours. It was so frustrating. I always sleep much better if I'm lying next to a girl, just hugging or spooning, but it's not exactly something the coaches would ever allow, even if it did mean I got a good night's sleep before the Olympic Games.

The next morning was an early one, as we were competing in the first subdivision together with teams from China, France and South Korea. I sat in the dining hall, half asleep, with my usual breakfast lined up in front of me – porridge with a blob of Nutella, a banana, some scrambled egg and orange juice – but I left most of it, forcing down what I could to give my body some energy and stop the churning in my stomach. It didn't work.

I was more scared that morning than I've ever been. This was the big one. Finals are one thing but qualifiers are far scarier. I knew that if I messed up on the pommel that day it was Games over, nineteen years of training straight down the drain. It was a horrible feeling.

All I could think was that in the next few hours my life would be defined.

In all my interviews and talks with the team leading up to London, I always said that there is nothing that can prepare you for an Olympic Games. It's something I realised in Beijing. Before then I'd competed in Europeans, World Championships and the Commonwealth Games, but nothing is as terrifying as an Olympic Games. It's unique. Which is why, as I sat staring at my porridge on that first morning, all I could think was that in the next few hours my life would be defined. My Olympic ambitions and everything that went with them might carry on to live for another day or they could be dead and buried by lunchtime. There was so much riding on it – the rest of my life, in fact. I drank what was left of my tea, told myself to ignore all those thoughts and headed back to the apartment to grab my stuff.

The team managers had decided we should get the early bus to the North Greenwich Arena to avoid the traffic and get there with plenty of time to prepare and get settled in. I was pretty stunned when 30 minutes later we walked into the arena and there were so many people there. For a first subdivision on the first day of competition, it was really unusual. I could see loads of people I recognised dotted around the crowd. My mum and my agent Gab were both there, as were my dad, Claude, and older brother, Leon.

Leon had been to watch me in one or two national competitions before, but this was the first international event he'd been to. His ticket was for a seat way up high in the stands but he's the kind of guy who'll still manage to turn up right at the front. He went up to a steward who

I knew that if I messed up on the pommel that day it was Games over, nineteen years of training straight down the drain. It was a horrible feeling.

was keeping an eye on the seats by the pommel and pointed me out, saying, 'That's my brother.' He must have given her a wink or something too, because she let him sit there. He loved it.

For my dad, seeing me compete live was a completely new experience. Before the Olympics he had only ever watched me on TV, so it was nice to give him the opportunity to see his son in competition. Gab had gone to meet him at King's Cross earlier that morning and because I don't see that much of my dad, it was the first time Gab had ever met him. That tells you quite a bit about the different roles my mum and dad have in my life. Gab and mum are so close now that I think she rings him almost as much as she does me.

Each team of five gymnasts was to rotate around all six pieces of apparatus that morning, with each gymnast looking to score as highly as possible on each one. Not only were we trying to help Great Britain get through to the team final but we also wanted to get as many gymnasts into the individual apparatus finals as possible, which you do by getting one of the top eight scores on that piece.

The pommel horse is obviously my speciality but that day it was the last thing we were going to compete on. The rings were first up, before the vault, then parallel bars, high bar, floor and finally, the pommel. I was due to sit out most of those because only four of the five gymnasts on the team have to perform on each piece and I'm not as good as the other guys, apart from on the pommel. I did compete on the high bar as well that day, but only after a lot of arguing with British Gymnastics about it before the Games.

They had wanted me to just compete on the pommel in team qualification, which would have meant waiting for practically the whole competition, before getting up to do my routine on the pommel, completely cold. In the lead up to the Games I argued my case, asking them to try and appreciate how nerve-shredding it is to have the kind of pressure that I have to perform on the pommel for five whole rotations, and to have to get up and just do it without a proper warm up.

Their problem was that letting me do another apparatus before the pommels meant that someone else wouldn't get to do it, someone who would probably score higher on it than me. But eventually, British Gymnastics backed down, saying I could compete on my second best piece – the high bar – on condition that I trained on it every day and did routines in practice. That was fine by me.

The high bar was two pieces before the pommels in qualification, so it gave me the chance to do my routine, get used to the noise from the crowd and clear my mind before the pressure was ramped right up. If I was going to make a mistake then I thought it was better to get it out of the way on the high bar than to risk in happening during my pommel horse routine.

And that was exactly what happened. I was doing my high bar routine fine in training, but when it came to the crunch in competition, I made a mistake and ended up scoring just 13.033, a score which put me almost rock bottom of the rankings.

The floor was next and it was a strong piece for us, with Kristian just missing out on a spot in the individual final. I was only half aware of all that though, because as that rotation ended we marched in line to the pommel horse. My stomach was in so many knots it was hard just to breathe.

I found a quiet place to sit down and draped my T-shirt over my head, blocking out the bright lights and distractions of the arena around me. In my mind I started going through my routine, picturing accurate hand placement, perfectly aligned limbs, pointed toes and a smooth, flowing rhythm throughout.

The person before me finished; I don't even know who it was – it might have been Max. It sounds weird, but at that point I couldn't care how he or the rest of the team had done on the pommel. I'd helped them all up until that point and now I needed to focus on what I had to do.

I do remember now – it *was* Max. He walked away from the pommel horse with a smile on his face and I said 'Good job.' But that was it,

I had to be completely selfish. I glanced over to the horse and saw Paul undoing the handles to move them into the right spot for me. Then I felt sick. I was scared.

In my head, I said a few words to my nan, as I always do before I compete, and got chalked up, smothering my hands in the white powder and rubbing them together, making sure the nervous moisture that had built up over the past hour was all absorbed. I stood at the corner of the mat and gave my arms a little shake, trying to rid the muscles of any lactic acid in them.

I saw the judges finish their writing up of Max's routine, jotting the scores down on their little pad. Then they were sitting there, waiting.

That's when I'm standing there, thinking, *Shit. It's coming up now. Shit.*

Max's score comes up on the screen.

Shit, now I've got even less time.

I look at it: 14.900.

Shit, that's a good score.

Then it's gone and my name flashes up in its place: Smith, Louis, with a big red stop sign positioned underneath. I know that in a minute that sign is going to change to green, meaning 'go', and then I'll have 30 seconds to prepare myself for the rest of my life.

It turns green. I blink slowly, then turn to the judges and give them a nice smile; *Please, judge me kindly.* I exhale deeply, trying to rid my body of the nerves, but it feels like World War III is kicking off in my stomach.

In my head, I said a few words to my nan, as I always do before I compete and got chalked up, smothering my hands in the white powder and rubbing them together.

Shit, let's just do it.

I walk, put my arms up, touch the pommel and then jump. Suddenly, it's happening. What were the nerves even about? Strange stuff goes through my head: *I wonder if anyone is recording this? How many of the judges are actually looking or are they too busy writing?* Really random stuff.

A difficult bit comes up and I tell myself: *Right, wait a minute. Concentrate. Oh, that was a good one, that was really good.*

Then another bit.

Slow, slow, slow, slow. Done. Yes, that was good, that looked really cool. Nearly there. Keep focusing. God, I'm really thirsty. Who's that shouting?

As soon as I go into the dismount the nerves come back – exactly the same feeling that I had before, and it's terrifying. I go into the dismount. I'm doing it. I'm doing it, then just before my hand goes out to land I feel sick.

Then, I'm down. Back on my feet. Within a split second my mind is overrun with thoughts:

Did I really just do that? For the last 50 seconds, did it really just go that perfect?

Every emotion had gone through me from the time we got to the pommel to landing my routine: nerves, fear, pride, joy, it was all there. And of course, there were the tears, I couldn't stop them coming. I have never had that feeling before in my life. It was sheer relief and a release of the tension that had been building up in me for years. In the stands, my mum was crying too and even Gab shed a tear, because they both knew the reasons why I hadn't been able to hold my emotions back any longer.

I walk, put my arms up, touch the pommel and then jump. Suddenly, it's happening.

With a score of 15.800 I had qualified for the pommel horse final in first place. It was just *so* satisfying to know that I had given myself the perfect opportunity to do a routine in the final. Everyone might have been expecting me to get to the final, but they don't understand how hit and miss gymnastics can be. Usain Bolt might false start once in a blue moon but you would always put your money on him reaching a 100m final – not much can go wrong from start to finish if he's fully fit. In gymnastics it's not like that; one misplaced thumb and it can all be over in a flash.

The record that Krisztian Berki and I have of making the finals of competitions is crazy; it's not normal in our sport. So to have given myself the chance of going for it one more time meant so much. That was it. I was in the Olympic final, where anything can happen, and it felt amazing.

On top of that, we had four other places in individual finals (Max on the pommel, Kris and Dan in the all-around and Kris again on the vault) and we had qualified in third place for the team final in two days' time. We had actually scored more points than China, the defending Olympic and world champions. It was a monstrous day for British Gymnastics, the best result for the British men in modern gymnastics history and we felt like there might be even better still to come.

Great Britain hadn't won a single medal in the team event since 1912 and the men had never won a team medal. So as far as I was concerned – and I made sure I told the boys – we had nothing to lose in the final. We had done what people expected us to do by qualifying and now the pressure was off.

On the day of the final, we bowled out into the arena as relaxed as it was possible to be in front of a crowd of people roaring their support for Team GB. It was the first time we had really heard that sort of noise and it surprised me at first; it's not something you ever really get in gymnastics.

Unlike in qualification, the pommel horse was our first piece of apparatus. It was to be my only routine of the competition, so I was determined to help get the team off to a good start with a decent score. I smashed it, scoring 15.966, the highest of everyone in the competition, which, together with good routines by Max and Dan, left us in second place after the first rotation, with only Ukraine ahead of us.

With the practical side of my job done, I was then able to concentrate on my role of team captain, which meant I could spend the rest of the competition getting behind the boys, keeping them in the right frame of mind and checking out what was going on with the other teams.

We were on rings next. It wasn't one of our best pieces but the crowd were really starting to get behind us and after each routine they got a little bit crazier. During Kristian's routine, I caught sight of one of the Japanese gymnasts landing on his knees after a vault – a rare mistake from them.

It wasn't only the Japanese; there were others messing up too. Nations like the USA who had qualified for the team final in first place and were one of the favourites for gold. We made it through the rings without any major mishaps and were fifth going into the third rotation, which took us to the vault.

Dan's vault was good enough to get a fist pump from his coach, but it was soon eclipsed by what Kristian did. His vault was a Yurchenko double pike, or a backwards double-somersault with straight legs in normal speak. Either way, Kristian nailed his landing and got the highest score of the competition: 16.550. The noise from the crowd was immense, it felt like the roof was about to blow off. We all gave Kristian high fives as he stepped off the runway and he cracked a little grin, but he was Mr Cool. Besides, there was plenty that could go wrong yet.

We had done what people expected us to do by qualifying and now the pressure was off.

We were in fourth spot before the parallel bars, with Russia, China and Japan ahead of us and the Americans, who were having a shocker, way down the rankings. Max was first up on the P-bars for us and went clean. I noticed Dan was getting a bit jittery before his routine, so I tried to ease the tension by cracking a couple of jokes. He made it through, as did Sam, who scored the highest of the three. We still hadn't messed anything up which, considering the mistakes happening around us from teams we considered to be better than we were, was almost unbelievable.

With two pieces of apparatus left, we were third behind China and Japan but no one was talking about medals yet. We didn't want to admit we were in with a shout in case we jinxed it. As it was, the next piece – the high bar – was where we messed up for the first time, when Sam missed a catch halfway through his routine, landing on his arse. I watched him re-chalk and walk back to the bar to finish, trying not to think about what that slip might have cost us.

Kristian was next up and stayed cool, smashing his routine again. When he landed, a little shiver went up my spine. With one of our strongest pieces – the floor – to come, there was still a slim chance we could sneak a medal.

But when the scores came up, I saw Ukraine had jumped ahead of us and thought, *Shit, this could be close, really close*. We were fourth with Russia and the USA, who were finishing strongly, trailing behind. I knew they were both still capable of beating us.

It was crunch time. The cameras gathered around us by the floor, ramming home the fact that we had a shot at reaching the podium. We still didn't talk about it, though. I didn't want to put any pressure on the boys, so I just told Dan, Max and Kristian to go out there and have fun, to make the most of the crowd and enjoy it. We all wanted to finish on a high, because apart from the one mistake on the high bar, we'd had almost the perfect competition.

'Whatever happens now, whether we finish second, fourth or sixth, we've done our job, and we've done it brilliantly.'

Max was first to perform on the floor and delivered, scoring 15.166 – a very good start. Then it was Dan's turn; another clean routine to earn 15.533. It was all going so well. Last to go was Kristian, our closer. I gave him a pat on the back to send him off, but I could tell he was already in his zone.

Soaking up all the nerves and pressure of being our last man of the day, Kristian was immense. He nailed it again, scoring 15.433 and the arena went completely mental. There were other teams still competing so I huddled the boys together and said, 'Whatever happens now, whether we finish second, fourth or sixth, we've done our job, and we've done it brilliantly.' As the scores got reeled off, we moved above Ukraine into second place, but Japan still hadn't finished on their last piece – the pommels.

Then, the unthinkable happened. Japan's star gymnast, three-time world champion, Kohei Uchimura, messed up his dismount. I was in shock. Uchimura's mistake meant Japan dropped down to fourth and we had a silver medal. I couldn't believe it. The crowd were making so much noise I could barely hear the guys speak and I couldn't find any words to say at all. It was beyond anything I, or any of us, had expected.

It was only a matter of minutes, though, before Japan launched a protest about Uchimura's score, saying his dismount was worthy of a higher mark. The words: 'Protest: Waiting' flashed up on the big screen, while we were still trying to come to terms with everything. We stood there for a minute or two staring at the screen in disbelief.

Then it started to sink in; we had a medal. Whatever happened, we had a team Olympic medal. The celebrating was back on for us then, while Japan and Ukraine, who were waiting to see if they would be bumped out of the medals completely, spent 15 painful minutes biting their nails.

Finally, 'Accepted' came up on the screen and Uchimura's new score was applied to the totals. Within seconds the order had flipped around; Japan had silver, we had bronze and Ukraine had nothing. It was hard for them, especially as their friends and family were sitting right behind the GB guys, who were all going crazy.

For us it was a case of nevermind the silver, we've got a bronze medal! A medal in the team event is unbelievable. In gymnastics, it's harder to get than an individual medal. For years we've been dominated by the Soviet Union, then Russia and Asia, so for us to come third was just mad.

In the press conference afterwards, everyone got a chance to answer questions about the team's performance, but it was nice, as team captain, to be able to make an overall conclusion and do a round-up of everything that had happened. It was a massive privilege for me to be part of that and represent the guys as team captain.

While Dan got hauled off for drug testing, the rest of us finished doing interviews before we headed back to Stratford, desperate for food. It was late so the entrance to the Village was dead quiet, except for the army guys on security duty who congratulated us, saying they had been listening to it all on the radio.

It's weird when you get back to the Village. It's a bit like walking into a bubble where you're not the only ones with medals and everyone else is preoccupied with preparing for the next day. We headed straight for the dining hall, all of us still on cloud nine. But it became very surreal, very quickly, when 10 minutes later it was just the five of us, sitting around a table, stuffing our faces. All we could think was, *Did that really just happen?*

I had five days to get my head around the fact that it was 30 July and I already had an Olympic medal, something I had been convinced could only happen on 5 August, the day of the pommel final, the day had been training as long as I can remember for. Those five days were quite chilled out, with bits of TV and sponsor work thrown in around brief training sessions. I would speak to my mum and Gab over the phone most days, but the conversations were all quite short and superficial. They'd ask stuff like, 'Have you done your washing?' or 'How's the wrist?' Nothing that might get me thinking about 'it'.

Gab remembers our last in-depth conversation before the Games as having been about six weeks before. We were on the phone and just got talking about it. We had a bit of a motivational chat and I remember him saying, 'In six weeks' time, you could be having the best night of your life.' But that was it, we didn't go too deep in any conversations after that.

There was one other phone call from Gab that I remember quite clearly, though. It came in that week or so in-between winning team bronze and the pommel final and it gave me a reason to be very excited about life beyond London 2012.

Not long before the Games we'd had a meeting with the *Strictly Come Dancing* team, who were looking for people to take part in the next series of the show, due to start not long after the end of the Olympics knew how big that would be for me. I'm a gymnast, not a footballer or an athlete, so to get onto something that big would be amazing. But was fairly sure that they would only want me if I was successful at the Olympics; if I flopped, I thought it would be game over.

So when Gab called to tell me they had signed me up, before my pommel final had even happened, I was over the moon. I just shouted out loud, I was so relieved that I would still have the opportunity to do something cool, even if I messed up in the final.

The pressure was still on, though. Despite the team bronze and the *Strictly* contract, if I didn't perform in the individual final I would see

Super Saturday was 4 August, the amazing night when Greg Rutherford, Jess Ennis and Mo Farah all won gold in the stadium. Our apartment was dead quiet that night though. It was just me and Max, who had also qualified for the pommel final, chilling. We played PlayStation, watched TV and packed our bags, making sure everything was in order for the next day. I did my usual thing of cracking jokes and staying relaxed when I was around Max; I didn't want him picking up on any of my nerves.

The next morning we did a little session in the Village, just a stretch and some resistance band work to warm up the muscles before getting some food. I loved the Caribbean stand in the dining hall, but my lunch that day went mostly untouched. My mind was alright but my stomach was flipping around again.

On the bus to the arena, I sat silently with my headphones on, just listening to music and trying to get in my zone. Paul says now that it worried him how quiet I was, because normally, before a competition, I'll be buzzing – laughing and joking around, even louder than I normally am. Not that day, though. I was completely quiet – the exact opposite to how Paul had seen me in ten years of taking me to competitions.

After the qualifiers, I had spoken to Paul about which routine I should do in the final. I had three options: my easy routine, the harder one or the hardest. I had been practising them all in training and they were all going well, so we decided we would make our final decision on the day, in the warm up.

We went into the warm-up gym and I sat on my own, with my headphones still on, until about 20 minutes before we went out into the arena and I jumped on the horse for my warm up. I always warm up the same way: jump up, lean side to side, wrist down, wrist down, leg in, leg out, leg in, leg out, circle, circle, circle, step back, circle, circle, circle, sit on the pommel, stretch, jump up and then off.

Most days when I'm doing that it all feels good, everything feels perfectly aligned and 'in the middle', as I put it. But there are some days when you're on the pommel and your equilibrium is just off. Everything feels a bit wrong. It's something you're never able to actually see, it's just a feeling.

That day, it all felt a bit off. I tried to do my hard routine and I just couldn't. It was weird. I was trying the hardest move – the triple Russian – and as soon as I started I was off balance. Off balance again and again and again. *Fuck,* I was thinking. Of all the days to have this feeling. It's something you might get once a week, when you're tired or distracted, so to have it then was . . . Well, it was a ball ache.

I was completely quiet – the exact opposite to how Paul had seen me in ten years of taking me to competitions.

Before that day I hadn't fallen during a routine for four weeks. When you consider how hit and miss gymnastics is and how hard my routine is, to have not made a single mistake in four weeks was like: 'He's ready.' So to then make a mistake six or seven minutes before I'm about to go into a final was a nightmare.

Paul walked over to me and asked if I was alright.

'I am so nervous,' was about all I could squeeze out.

He tried to put me at ease, saying, 'You've done this routine so many times. You've done a million circles. This is just another one – one more routine. Just go and do it.'

He was clearly worried I was going to crack and go to pieces.

I decided there was no way I could do my hardest routine, because if I did and messed it up, I'd be thinking I knew I shouldn't have gone for it. But I also wasn't going to bottle it completely and do my easy routine. So I decided on the medium routine, which was less risky than the one I kept messing up in the warm up.

Normally, when Paul walks into a competition with me, he says it feels like he's walking out with one of the gladiators into the arena, that he's

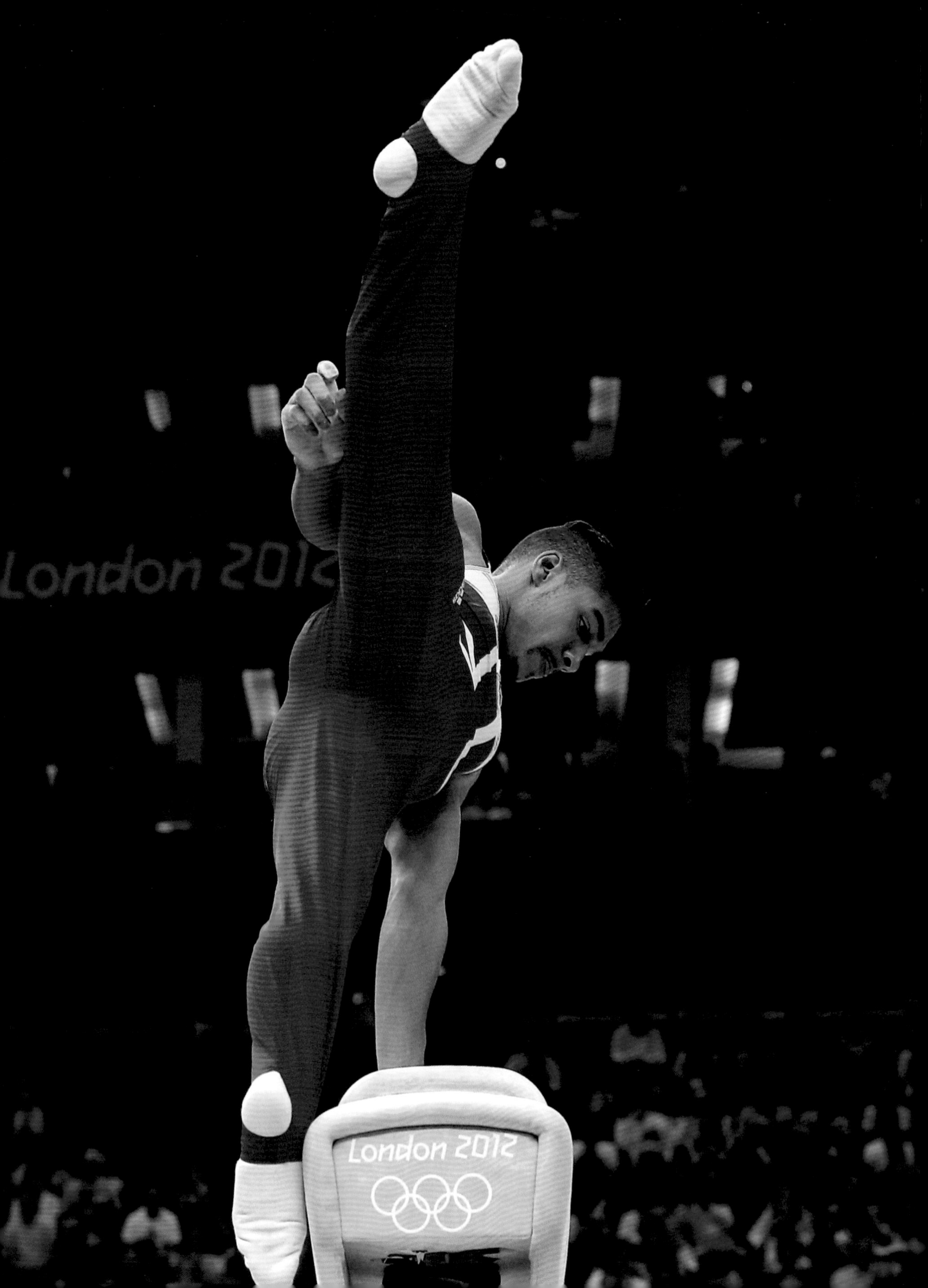
London 2012
London 2012

just there for show and I'm there to get the job done. But in London that day, he says he felt like I was one of the Christians about to be fed to the lions and he was walking in behind me thinking, *I'm not sure he's going to get through this.*

I was the last of the eight gymnasts to perform on the pommel, which meant I knew all their scores before I did my routine. But I didn't watch anyone else, I just sat there, going through my routine in my head, trying to block everything else out.

When I went up into my first handstand I could feel my arms shaking. This was everything. The next 50 seconds were what it had all come down to. *Don't mess up now.* Then muscle memory just took over and before I knew it my feet were on the floor and my arms were in the air. It was the best I had ever performed that routine in months and months of training. Under that pressure, on such a massive occasion, I'm still not quite sure how I did it.

When I landed I knew I was in with a chance of gold, but the score that flashed up matched Berki's 16.066, which had been etched on my brain as the one I needed to beat. I thought it was going to be close, but I'd hoped that with a home crowd, and on home soil, I might just edge it.

When I landed I knew
I was in with a chance of gold.

and the code favours the execution over the difficulty rating. So even though I had done a harder routine, Berki got the gold.

At the time, I took it on the chin. I wanted Berki to get his dues for taking a gold medal back to Hungary – he deserved it. They were both fantastic routines. And in every interview I did leading up to the Olympics I always said that all I wanted was to do my routine clean, and then whatever happens, happens. That was exactly how it turned out.

When I went into the press conference afterwards, all the journalists were asking if I was disappointed and did I think I should have won gold. I tried to drill it into them that I had just won Olympic silver, and they were asking if I was pissed off! Gymnastics isn't a sport where Britain normally wins gold and suddenly we had this silver medal which stuck out like a sore thumb. This was the best Olympic medal we'd had, just accept it. I tried to tell them I was a happy man. I had Olympic silver and two Olympic bronze medals in my collection at the age of 23. And I'm a gymnast!

I did eventually get round to watching Berki's routine on TV, a few months after the Games and technically, I'm not sure his routine was so sharp – his spindle was piked and on his Wu travel, his legs weren't great. Don't get me wrong, I'm not bitter. I'm still happy with the silver medal and the way my life is going but, you know, it stings a little bit. I'm only human.

The night after the pommel final wasn't as drunken as people might expect. Aston met me at Team GB house in Stratford, where we had some champagne, and we did hit Aura later that night, but I think I only managed about two drinks in the club. There were so many people coming up to me all night that I didn't have time for many more.

I made up for it the week after. During the day I'd have bits of media and sponsor things to do, then we'd go out to clubs and bars in the evenings, get back to the Village at about five in the morning, eat and be in bed by 5.45 a.m. Then it was up again in 10 minutes to do breakfast television. Those mornings were painful.

I made it to the following Sunday in one piece, just about. It was the day of the closing ceremony and me, Sam and Max decided to take our scooters with us to the stadium. We'd bought them in Westfield not long after we got to the Village, just because the place was so big we didn't want to walk everywhere, and wanted to save our legs.

It was really far from the Village to the stadium so we scooted there. We were spotted by a Gamesmaker on the way in who said, 'You can't take them in.'

'It's okay, we're leaving them with some friends who are waiting for us by the stadium.'

That was a complete lie. We folded them up when we got to the stadium and hid them under our Team GB jackets. They were sticking out everywhere, but in the crowd no one could really spot them. We made our way right to the front, walked down the steps into the stadium and just before we got to the pack of photographers, whipped the scooters out and scooted onto the track – it made for some great pictures in the papers the next day.

It was a good night, with the Team GB after-party in the Village carrying on until really late, loads of food and drink, and everyone celebrating the end of the Games. I'll admit it was a drunken night. I think I made it to bed at about six in the morning.

When I woke up, the Village was practically deserted. Most people had packed up and got on buses already. Apart from the rowers, who were still trying to get their boats loaded onto these big lorries, everyone had gone. I felt sad. I was also hungover and had loads of packing to do.

None of the buses that had been laid on to drop people at certain points, so they could either be met by family or get onto transport home, were of any use to me. I needed to get back to Peterborough, so had planned to get the train from King's Cross until I realised just how much stuff I had. I ended up getting a cab all the way home. Not that I remember the journey – I think I was asleep for most of it.

I couldn't wait to get home by then. I'd been away for weeks and weeks – at a training camp in Lilleshall, then to France for the prep camp and then at the Olympics. It was so nice to walk in the door, flop on the sofa and just do nothing – apart from make the short trip to Mum's for dinner, that is. Some things you just can't match, even in an Olympic-sized food hall.

9

Sunshine, *Strictly* and spray tans

Much as I loved being back at home after the Olympics, I was really, really excited about my post-Games holiday to Marbella. It was something I'd set up months earlier for me, my friends and my teammates to spend some time together after the Games. Now, with all the stress and tension finally gone, I could really relax and enjoy myself, knowing that I'd done myself, my coach and my mum proud.

Why Marbs? I'd been there for a week's holiday in the summer of 2011 and it was amazing. The worst thing about it was that I had to leave early to be home by a certain date for training.

The vibe there is just awesome, the women are beautiful and everyone's there to do one thing: party. It's not like those places you see on the 'uncovered' TV programmes where people are going into nightclubs in shorts and vests, getting drunk and ending up naked in the street. It's a bit nicer. I don't really like those types of holidays; they're a bit too crazy for me. Marbs is more of a toned-down version. It's more about having fun, and going out in jeans and a shirt as opposed to a pair of shorts and flip-flops.

I set it up so that me and a group of my mates flew out first, and then my teammates came out a bit later. When the first group of us left – I think there were fifteen lads all together – it was a week after the closing ceremony so I was definitely well rested and ready for another party.

It's the first holiday I can remember where I was able to chill out completely and do what I wanted without having to worry about staying in shape or getting back home for training.

Even when I was younger, before the days when the words 'Olympic' and 'medal' had been burned into my brain, we never really went abroad that much. Most of our holidays were in this country. It was cheaper and easier to stay in the UK because we usually took my nan who couldn't travel that far. Hunstanton in Norfolk was the place we went to most, but when I got to about 12 years old, even that holiday was impossible to fit into my schedule. By then I was training most of the time, and if I wasn't training I was competing, so we didn't go on holiday at all when I was between the ages of about 12 and 18.

Marbs was easily the best holiday I'd ever been on.

The whole holiday was like a complete release for me, really. After the immense pressure of the years leading up to the Olympics and then the past month, which had been the most intense experience of my life, Marbs was exactly what I needed.

By the end of it, I was pretty broken. There hadn't been much sleeping and I wasn't used to partying for ten days straight, so I was massively ready to go home, back to my own bed and spend some quality time in front of *Call of Duty*.

I only had a day to recover before I was due at my first *Strictly* session, so I was probably still detoxing when I met everyone. But luckily, that first gathering was mostly about meeting all the other celebrities who are taking part in the show, so nothing that required too much energy on my part.

We also filmed the launch trailer that they would use on TV to reveal which celebrities were taking part. My role in that was mostly sitting on

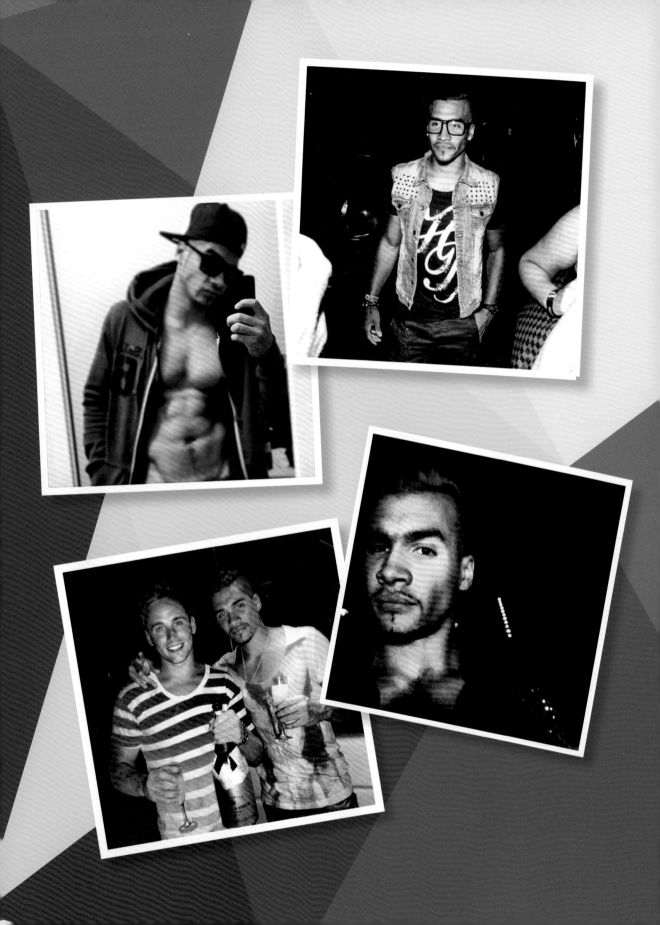

a sofa with Fern Britton and Nicky Byrne from Westlife – oh, and giving a cheeky little wink to the camera. It was a deceptively gentle introduction to what would turn out to be a tough 13 weeks in the spotlight.

I was meeting most of the other celebrities for the first time that day, although I did know the cyclist Victoria Pendleton from seeing her at sponsor events and I had met Dani Harmer before because we'd worked on some *Blue Peter* stuff together. But I was looking forward to getting to know everyone else. I always believe in the saying 'you should never judge a book by its cover', so I didn't go into it with any preconceived ideas of what the others would be like. Gab did though, in terms of their dancing skills, that is. I rang him after that first session and told him Denise Van Outen and Kimberley Walsh from Girls Aloud were gonna be on the show, and all I heard down the phone was: 'Shit, shit, shit.' He knew they'd both be amazing dancers and could see that Glitterball Trophy moving further and further away.

When Gab had told me during the Olympics that they wanted me on the programme I was so excited, because I always wanted to do something fun after the Games. When you do one of the smaller sports that doesn't get as much publicity as things like football or athletics, the Olympics gives you a unique opportunity – if you do well – to do something fun once it's over.

A lot of the reality shows on TV aren't always the best, but I think *Strictly* is a bit different to most of them. It shows you working hard and focusing on a goal, rather than a show like *Big Brother* where you're just sitting around in a house; even the most saint-like person has faults that will come out in that kind of situation.

I had lots of chats in the gym with Paul about what I might do if I took some time out after the Olympics and we'd talked about all sorts. He was down on most of the things I'd suggest, saying, 'Don't do that, it's for the end of your career, not the beginning,' but when *Strictly* came up as an option he was all for it. That was when I knew it was definitely something worth doing.

Gab had wanted me to do *Strictly* for ages, but he knew that the Olympics would obviously play a part in any decisions the producers made. The producers seemed to like me, though, and they came to watch me compete during the Games, so they knew I would do my best to put on a good show. I knew I had rhythm and could move well, so before it started I thought I could maybe make it through to the last few weeks of the series, but I never thought I would do as well as I did.

I think I was one of the favourites to win it right from the beginning, just

I thought I could maybe make it through to the last few weeks of the series, but I never thought I would do as well as I did.

because people presumed that as a gymnast, I would be a great dancer. But to be completely honest, I know a lot of gymnasts who wouldn't have made it past the first week of the show – loose hips and an ability to move to a beat aren't things you ever really need as a male gymnast.

Apparently, I've always had good rhythm. Mum still has an old school report of mine from when I was in year seven – so I would have been about 12. It was from a combined dance/drama class that we had to do a couple of times a week and in it the teacher calls me an exceptional dancer, someone who moves with 'a sophistication beyond his years'. Although she also says I did it without a great deal of effort and preparation, two things I would definitely need if I were going to succeed on *Strictly*.

It wasn't really the dancing I was worried about; my main concern was that I might have to pull out through injury before I had a chance to get going. I didn't think my body would survive 13 weeks of training and performing. It's tough, especially if injury-wise you're not in the best shape, and with my knee and back both needing to be handled with care, it was a worry.

Even quite early on, when everyone was knackered from the group training sessions we did at the beginning, I was the one limping out. I was spending more time doing the kind of cardiovascular training that I didn't really do much of in gymnastics and my knee was suffering from the impact of that. My back is just an annoying niggle that's always there, although it's always worse when the weather gets cold – I'm like a 60-year-old. I think all the sports people who go into the programme have some sort of ache or pain; Michael Vaughan had problems with his knee. But everyone thinks that because you're an Olympian or a sportsman, you are in prime condition.

My broken body meant I needed a partner who would persevere with me when I needed breaks from training and one who would be willing to compromise. I was so, so lucky to end up dancing with Flavia, who did both of those things. It took a couple of weeks, but she developed a great understanding of what I could and couldn't do.

At first she was like, 'Let's go, let's do it, fifty routines, come on.' And I just couldn't. So she had to realise that although I was an athlete who had been in the shape of his life a month ago, you don't come out of the Olympics in top shape, you come out wrecked. Once she got that, she was the best partner I could have wished for.

Although I had watched the programme before, I'd never been able to sit and watch a whole series so I didn't really know who the dancers were or which one I might work with best. Of course, I knew who Bruce

Forsyth was and Craig Revel Horwood, because he was like the Simon Cowell figure, but that was about it. But by the time they paired me up with Flavia, I had already met her and danced with her while learning the group dance for the premier night, though I hadn't known then that she would end up being my partner.

When they put us together during that first show I was really pleased because we had done quite a few bits together in that group dance. We had even done a little lift and she'd just felt like a good partner to me. It did take me a while to get used to the touchy-feely world of dancing, though; I'm not naturally a very touchy-feely, grabby kind of guy, unless I know someone really well and am comfortable with them.

I was so, so lucky to end up dancing with Flavia.

Paul, who knows me better than most people, was laughing watching me on TV with Flavia when we were first paired up because there was no physical contact between us at all and I just walked off stage behind her. He called me afterwards and said, 'Louis, you've spent your whole career marching into competitions behind a pretty girl carrying a flag; you don't have to do it anymore. Now you have to grab her and hold her.' It's just not the way I am; not with someone I've only met a handful of times before, anyway.

But as soon as I'd had the chance to spend a bit of time with Flavia, I knew she was the right person for me to work with. She didn't have the same mindset as everyone else, who, when it came to dancing, would get really serious and strict. She was just very smiley and happy; like a breath of fresh air. It's just the way she is. Although she wants to do well in the competition, she always makes sure that her partners enjoy their time on Strictly. Although it's hard and she worked me hard, she wanted me to enjoy myself, too.

If it hadn't been for Flavia, I would never have survived as long as I did – let alone win it. I'm not the easiest person to work with or coach, and

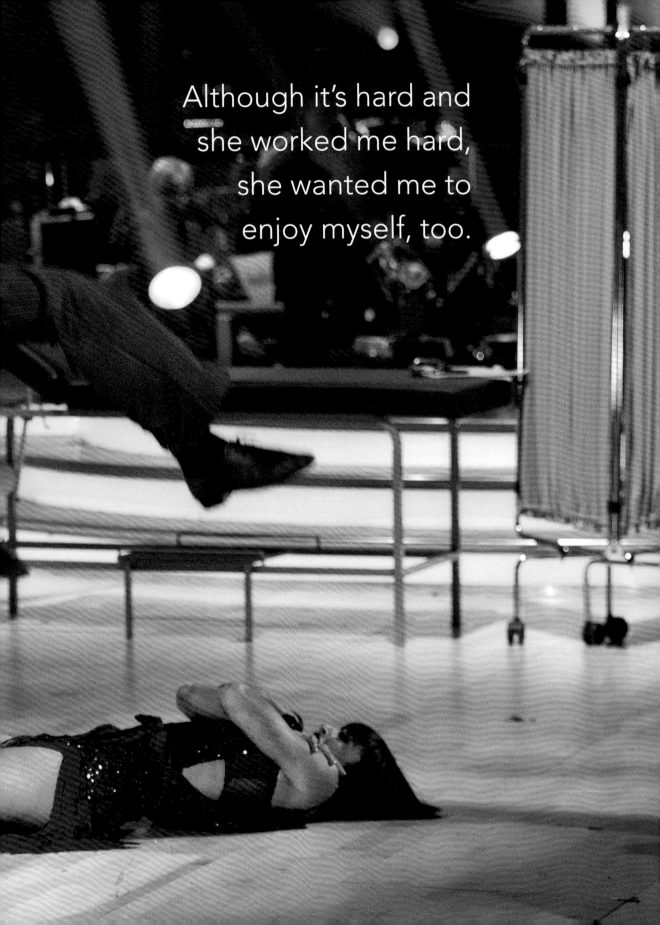

Although it's hard and
she worked me hard,
she wanted me to
enjoy myself, too.

I know that I can frustrate people who are trying to get the best out of me. I probably had to have more breaks than anyone on the show, but she never lost her patience or threw a diva-like strop with me in all the time we spent together, which is pretty impressive.

She was still strict with me when she needed to be, but at the same time she could tell when I needed a break and she knew when I needed to let loose and just mess around for 10 minutes. Most importantly, we actually got on really well. She's such a nice, chilled-out person that it was easy to spend hours and hours with her every day, which isn't always the case with all the couples on the show.

It's mad. Just call me Patrick Swayze.

It was at one of our first rehearsals that I heard Flavia admit that she thought we could do well. She was doing a piece to camera and even though we hadn't even done our first dance yet, she said we had a chance of winning. I knew it would be a long haul though, and just like with the Olympics, I would never assume anything – I didn't want to jinx it.

Our first dance was the Cha Cha. It sounded simple: one, two, cha-cha-cha; one, two, cha-cha-cha. Sadly, it wasn't as simple as it sounded and I found it really hard. I think we all did. It was so different to anything we'd ever done before. I remember trying to get the hip movement right and it felt so awkward. The cameras caught me telling Flavia that I felt like a woman who couldn't dance at a party and that was exactly it. I was trying to do the sexy, flamboyant thing but it was hard when all my life I'd been instructed not to show my emotions and to focus and concentrate. Now all of a sudden I was being told to wiggle my hips and smile. I was definitely out of my comfort zone.

But when it came to performing, I loved it. It was such a buzz and the crowd gave us a standing ovation, which I really wasn't expecting. Of all the judges it was Darcey Bussell who seemed most impressed.

'I wasn't expecting that rhythm . . . you've worked hard on that hip action, I can tell. In my eyes I think you're gonna go far in this show.'

I got called a 'snake hipped wonder' by Bruno Tonioli, too, but Len Goodman said it wasn't a gold medal performance and needed to be a bit crisper. Craig was harder to impress, too. He said my performance was a bit awkward at times and that I looked too serious. Still, we did well for our first week, scoring 27 out of 40, so I was really pleased.

That went up to score 30 out of 40 the following week when we did a waltz to 'Puppy Love', another performance Bruno seemed to enjoy. But week three was when things really, really took off. We were doing a salsa to the song '(I've Had) The Time of My Life' from the film, *Dirty Dancing*, which I've never seen so I had no idea the reaction it was going to get.

I knew it was a big film and that people love it but I just thought it was a bit of a cult thing, like *Grease*. We received an unbelievable amount of messages after that performance, from girls saying they were in tears watching it and that they wanted to be the girl being lifted up at the end. I just didn't get it at all. I had to do the same routine on the *Strictly* tour that we took around the country at the start of 2013, too, but with one of the other dancers, Ola Jordan, because Flavia was doing her own show in the West End. We did that lift 31 times in about a month and it won us the trophy almost every night of the whole tour. It's mad. Just call me Patrick Swayze – well, the more tanned version.

In the main show, it was definitely the biggest response I'd had so far to any of my dances; even Craig liked it. Len was still a bit critical, saying that although I'd done the lift excellently, the performance was a bit too timid for him. The booing he got for saying that was almost deafening so I knew the crowd were into it, and my phone went mental with all the Twitter mentions about the dance, so I knew everyone watching at home was, too.

It was the week after that when I messed up big time. Not on stage – our Halloween Tango was wicked. I got to dress up like a zombie with some funky contact lenses that made my eyes look really freaky and we scored the first 9s of the competition. Bruno, Darcey and Len all gave us 9 out of 10 for the zombie tango and Darcey said it was the best tango

of the night. When we topped the leader board with 35 points I was totally shocked.

I put what happened next partly down to those heightened emotions, I wasn't thinking straight. The dance-off between the bottom two couples is always filmed on the same night as the main programme, so even though the public don't find out who's left the show until the following day, we all know on the day of the show. In the Halloween show, the dance-off was between Sid Owen and Colin Salmon and it was Sid who went.

By then we'd all got to know each other really well and become good mates, so it was sad to see people leaving. I was gutted and, without thinking, tweeted how I was feeling: 'Wat an amazing but emotional roller coaster. So much luv for @FlaviaCacace & it's so sad to say bye to @sidowen5 and @TheOlaJordan #crewlove.'

About 10 seconds after I'd tweeted, Gab got a phone call from the *Strictly* press officer who just shouted down the phone at him, 'Get Louis to take down that tweet, immediately.' As he hung up the phone from her it rang again – it was me, 'Gab, you're not gonna believe what I've just done.'

As soon as I tweeted it, I realised what I'd done. *Shit!* It could only have been up there for about 30 seconds but that was long

enough. Gab got another call from the producer this time and it was in all the papers the next day. It's weird, because I knew not to do it but in the heat of everything – with the emotions and adrenaline – it just happened.

There were two weeks left to get through before the big live show at Wembley, which I really wanted to make it to. Wembley was like a marker; to make it that far in the series would be amazing. But our chances took a slight hit when our samba failed to impress the judges. I was finding the Latin dances much harder to pick up than the ballroom, so I wasn't that surprised the scores were a bit lower, but I thought it was a little harsh of Darcey to say she was disappointed with me – it's not like I wasn't trying!

'Cancel absolutely everything. I can't do it. I can't do this anymore.'

The week before Wembley was the halfway point of the competition and I was determined to better our samba score with a waltz that would impress the judges. It worked on all of them except for Craig, who called it pedestrian and said I needed to act the dance more. I thought a fight was going to break out between him and the others when he only gave us a 6 and they gave us three 9s, but it was enough to get us through to Wembley which was all I was worried about.

It was around that time that everything started to get on top of me a bit. The show was ramping up, I needed to put more hours into training and I was doing loads of media work as well, with sponsor commitments and appearances most nights of the week. I would end up doing 14-hour days. I'd get up really early to get an 8 a.m. train down to London from Peterborough, do a photo shoot for a couple of hours, then go to training and do seven or eight hours with Flavia. Then I'd be straight out to an event in the evening and get back to my room about midnight.

Then the next day I'd have to do it all over again. It got to the point when nothing was going in my head at all during training and I would get so frustrated with myself because what Flavia was showing me was easy, I just couldn't do it. It would drive me up the wall. And this was the week before Wembley.

After Wembley I said to Gab: 'Cancel absolutely everything. I can't do it. I can't do this anymore. This isn't just some silly little side thing that you can learn without thinking; you have to have a clear head.'

I couldn't keep working and train properly at the same time. And I didn't want to go out there looking like a piece of crap because Flavia had high expectations of me, and the rest of the country did as well. So I had to perform. And I couldn't do that with the way that everything was going.

I wasn't pleased with my performance at Wembley at all, but it wasn't down to my hectic schedule in the end. The night before the show, we were doing our rehearsals and the big bosses decided our American Smooth routine wasn't working for the cameras, so the floor manager asked us to change things around. 'Just move that bit there, take this bit out, move that bit around. . . .'

After what had been a stressful week anyway, it wasn't ideal to change the whole thing the night before the show. I think we got to dance it once more before the live performance and, even that time, we only made it about 10 seconds into the routine before we got lost and messed up the steps. It didn't exactly fill me with confidence ahead of performing on our biggest stage yet.

You know that phrase 'It'll be alright on the night'? It wasn't. We got the steps wrong and it was all a bit of a nightmare. It did my head in and I did think we might leave the show that week. It wasn't the only time I thought that – I thought it later on, in the semi-final, too – but it was a very different fear then. At Wembley I was scared because I knew I hadn't done my best, so if I'd left I would have been devastated. I didn't want my *Strictly* experience to end when I knew I hadn't given it my absolute best.

I was so relieved when we survived, but the next week we were down again. The judges said my Paso Doble was lacking attitude and fight, and told me I needed to really let go of my emotions, to act the dances. I was finding that the most difficult part of it all and it was frustrating because I was working hard to get the dancing right, but still I had Craig saying, 'You can go no further with us unless you give yourself up.'

For someone who's been trained in gymnastics for the past nineteen years, it was hard to break out of the way it teaches you to be, which is quite rigid and almost a bit wooden. The judges wanted me to relax and play up to the cameras and it took me a while to get my head around being like that.

No matter how many times we practised it, she still screamed every time.

After the Paso Doble week, though, the *Strictly* producers called in an acting coach as a bit of a gimmick for the training video, but we actually worked with him for a couple of hours and it really did help me. We did these stupid little exercises, screaming in each other's faces and stuff, to try and loosen me up – it was quite strange. But it taught me to let go and not be so serious.

It was exactly what I needed for the Charleston, which is a really fun, playful dance, so the performance part of it would be 'make or break'. It felt really good when we performed it and the judge's reactions told me that it looked good, too. I think Len's response, 'Shut up, close the door and call me Mary! I'm telling you Louis, you've got a personality and you've come out and shown it,' was probably my favourite, but Bruno's 'the making of a true contender' was an amazing comment too.

It was such a fun dance to do, especially the bit where I did a flip and landed by Flavia's head. No matter how many times we practised it, she still screamed every time; I'd just hear this 'Arrrghh' as my feet came down.

I always know where my body is so I wasn't worried at all, but it was very funny that she was so nervous about it.

That week seemed to give us the momentum we needed and our tango/rumba fusion dance went down just as well on the following show. I don't think it was just because Darcey got distracted by my arms, either. So we were in the semi-finals, and as the last man standing in the competition and one surrounded by some truly incredible dancers, by then I really felt like I had nothing to lose.

When our first dance – the Jive – didn't go down as well as we'd hoped, I knew I'd have to do a flawless foxtrot to make it through to the final. Performing under pressure is what I'm used to and we smashed it, scoring 39, the highest of the series so far for a foxtrot. Len called me a true sportsman – one who had been knocked down and come back stronger – and I couldn't have asked for a much better compliment than that.

I'd spoken with Flavia already about what we might do for our show dance if we made it to the final and we both agreed we wanted to do something completely different – something that had never really been done on the show before. Flavia chose the music, which was Take That's 'Rule the World', because it fitted with her vision of doing something very powerful. We thought it would be good to do a dance that was similar to what you see in the circus when people are balancing on each other, something that really showed how well strength and elegance can come together.

I knew for a week or so before the semi-final that if we made it to the last show I'd be going topless, because it fitted in with our contemporary theme, so I decided to get myself into better shape in time for that. I went on a bit of a diet, eating only porridge and fruit for breakfast and during the day things like couscous, lentils, chicken or fish. Then in the evening I had just chicken and vegetables or fish and vegetables – no carbohydrates at all. It was a boring diet, but it worked.

I started doing a little workout circuit in my room, too. I bought an exercise bike and would do an intense 45-minute session when I got back from dance training every night in the week leading up to the final. After a nine-day healthy eating and exercising crash course, I definitely looked in better shape – everyone who saw my 'before' and 'after' photos thought I'd Photoshopped them.

I ended up getting my first ever spray tan in the week before the final. Not because I wanted one, but because everyone – *everyone* – on the show had spray tans. Everyone apart from Johnny Ball, anyway. They'd all have one before the show every week and I was always the only contestant that didn't, so they were constantly on at me. 'Louis, why don't you get a spray tan? It'll look good, and give you a glow, make you look healthy.'

We didn't want people to be sitting there scratching their heads and wondering what on earth we were doing.

They bugged me about it week after week after week and each time I was like, 'No, I don't need it. Look at me, I'm already tanned.' On the rehearsals day before the semi-finals the spray tan people were in again and said, 'Come on Louis, the show's finishing soon, just have one spray tan.' So I promised that if I made the final I'd have one.

That was how I ended up standing in my pants in a little booth, being sprayed with fake tan the day before the *Strictly* final. I only had the lightest version, so you couldn't really tell until I pulled my pants waistband down. It smelt nice, though – that was the plus side.

If you had asked me that week whether I thought I could win *Strictly*, I would have said no. I honestly didn't feel like I was technically the best dancer left in the show. I knew we had something quite different in our show dance, which was good, but it also worried us a bit. What if people didn't get it? It was so different to what everyone else has done for the show dance on *Strictly* in the past; we didn't want people to be sitting there scratching their heads and wondering what on earth we were doing.

We knew that people were expecting somersaults and backflips from me, so it was a big gamble to go for almost the opposite of that. But that was what we needed to do, especially as I wasn't the most technical dancer there and everyone else was going to be doing loads of lifts and crazy, complicated routines.

On the morning of the final it looked even less likely that we would win. I'd been having physiotherapy and regular massage in the week leading up to the final, but on the Saturday I woke up, my back was in bits. There was no way I could do the dress rehearsal and the *Strictly* guys said they couldn't get me a masseur until two o'clock that afternoon, so I rang Gab and asked if there was anything he could do.

I think he rang round every masseur in London before he eventually found someone, but I still couldn't manage the full dress rehearsal. Flavia didn't panic, though, and I knew that as long as I kept moving during the day and didn't stress it too much, my back ought to be ok.

We made it through the *Dirty Dancing* Salsa routine without any problems and the judges even said it was better than it had been the

first time. Then it was show time. Well, show dance time. We were the last ones to perform, so we'd seen how amazing everyone else was, but we also knew how incredible the contrast would be between the high tempo flashiness in the others' dances and the flowing elegance of ours.

The judges loved it, and gave us a perfect score – 40 out of 40. Len even said he didn't think they'd see a show dance as magical as that if the show went on for another twenty years. I was so, so happy, but I was starting to feel my back getting stiff again so I had to ask someone to get me a heat pack. When we were standing in the studio with Tess Daly and all the other celebrities and dancers, I had one arm behind my back; it was holding the heat pack in place that I was hoping would allow me to finish our third and final routine of the show. It was touch and go right up to the last minute, but it's amazing what adrenaline can get you through. In my case it was three more flips in the Charleston – and more screams from Flavia after each one.

When we were standing in the line-up waiting for Bruce and Tess to read out the results of the final, I was pretty relaxed because no matter whose name they read out, I'd had a brilliant time. I'd made it to the end and whatever happened next, I was happy with myself. I knew I had a one in three chance of winning but I still wasn't expecting it to be me. When you know that the two other people there are better than you, then you just take things in your stride. If you win, you win, but if you don't, then happy days, it doesn't matter.

When they said our names, we were both in shock. For the next few hours Flavia just kept looking at me, wide-eyed saying, 'I can't believe we've won.' I was half joking when I said on the show that it was nice to be able to finally say I'd won something in 2012, but it was. Okay, it wasn't the dream I'd been chasing since the age of four, or the reason I'd spent countless hours putting my body through hell in the gym, but it was still something I'd worked hard for and had put my all into from the very beginning. And it wasn't only for me, it was for Flavia too, which made it even more worthwhile.

10

A design for life

As happy as I was to win the *Strictly* Glitterball Trophy, the end of the show meant a few weeks' rest for me – and my back – before the *Strictly Come Dancing* Live Tour started. It was a chance for me to finally sit back and take in what a year 2012 had turned out to be. Having gone from the Olympics, to Marbs and then straight into *Strictly*, I didn't feel like I'd really been able to do that yet.

Not everyone was pleased about it, though. Mum was devastated that *Strictly* was over. She kept asking, 'What am I going to do on Saturday nights now?' As if she thought I'd be on the show forever. It had always been my nan's favourite programme and Mum always said I reminded her of her dad when I was in hold with Flavia, as he and nan used to ballroom dance a lot when they were younger, so I think it had been quite an emotional experience for her to watch me on there.

The break meant no more photo shoots for a while, too. I'd done so many while *Strictly* was going on, to help promote the programme and my part in it, that it was nice to think I could chill out for a bit and finally eat all the pizza I'd been dreaming about for weeks.

The photo shoots were all good fun, but they were very different to the ones I'd been used to doing posing in my gym kit on a pommel horse. Not that I ever knew what the *Strictly* ones were going to be like until the morning of the shoot, when Gab would pick me up from King's Cross station. I'd get in the car and he'd say:

'Right, you've got a shoot today with *Reveal/Heat/Cosmopolitan* magazine. It's a naked one.'

'What?'

'It's a naked one.'

'What d'you mean?'

'You've gotta be naked.'

'What, fully naked? '

'Well . . .'

'Thanks for telling me, Gab. I'd have started my diet plan a bit earlier if I'd known that.'

There were a couple of magazine spreads towards the end of 2012 where I was wearing fewer clothes than I normally would in public,

including one where I was holding a champagne bottle with a popping cork. And another one for *Cosmopolitan* where I was holding a gym pose minus the leotard, but it was to raise awareness for a cancer charity, so it was for a good cause.

They're not that bad to shoot as long as it's not cold and there isn't a room full of people standing around and gawping. I think there were only two girls in the room when I did the champagne bottle shoot – the photographer and the photographer's assistant who was doing the lighting and other stuff. It's not like you need a stylist when you're naked. Whenever I do a shoot like that, though, I end up seeing the picture everywhere, for ages afterwards. I don't keep copies of the photos, but they're the pictures people always bring when they want me to sign something. It's strange. I don't really feel like a sex symbol, but people do seem to like those pictures.

Strictly had clearly taken things to a whole new level of madness. Before the show, I was well known for being an Olympic gymnast, but now I was becoming a bit of a celebrity, too, and that was a whole new world to me. And an alien world, at that.

It's one where the tabloids are constantly trying to find dirt on you, and when they can't, they'll just print the most ludicrous stories they can think of. Before the Olympics, I was someone they tried to protect and promote in a good light, but afterwards it all just became quite vicious – it was something I wasn't used to at all.

They went chasing after Billie, the girlfriend I'd broken up with almost two years before, and twisted her words to try and cause trouble between us. I still see her now and again and we get on really well, so there wasn't a story there at all.

But the stupidest thing I read was that I had left my girlfriend to start going out with Kimberley Walsh from Girls Aloud. I didn't even have a girlfriend at the time, but apparently I split up with her because I fancied Kimberley who I'd been on *Strictly* with. The same Kimberley whose boyfriend I knew well and got on with. The whole thing came out of one interview where I was asked whether I thought Kimberley was pretty and I answered that yes, she was a very beautiful girl. And that was enough for them to create that entire story; it was crazy.

There was also the ridiculous story about two *Playboy* girls who I met in a bar. Somehow they ended up back in my room – a bit like one of those bad smells that follows you home from a night out. I was a bit drunk so I wasn't going to throw them out if they wanted to spoon or have a cuddle, but they obviously wanted me to try it on with them and when it didn't happen they were pissed off. They wanted something to tell the papers, so they made something up about me showing them my hair straighteners and making them watch videos of *Strictly* on my phone. It was all quite funny really, but none of it makes me regret doing *Strictly* at all; it's just like the baggage that comes with it.

I was well known for being an Olympic gymnast, but now I was becoming a bit of a celebrity, too, and that was a whole new world to me.

The only reason people began to know about me in the first place was because of my success in gymnastics, so it's not something I'm ever going to complain about. And I know that the only way I can play a part in keeping the legacy from the Games going and help gymnastics to build a bigger audience is to make the most of the opportunities – like *Strictly* – that do come my way.

People like Jess Ennis and Mo Farah don't have to really do much to keep themselves in the public eye; they've won gold at the Olympics in a sport that everyone knows and loves. But I'm in a bit of a different situation. I've got a lot more work to do before gymnastics is established in the same way as athletics in this country.

Even before the Beijing Olympics, I knew that if I went there and did really well, then people would know who I was for a while, but that it would

fizzle out pretty quickly. The only people who would really remember me are quite a specific group – people in the world of gym and those who are fanatical about sport. So I needed something that would fix my face in people's minds. Something so memorable that when they saw me they would say, 'Oh yeah, it's that gymnast, Louis Smith.'

That was when I decided to do something a bit wacky with the hairstyle, and keep changing it to keep it fresh and different. I'm not stupid or naïve. Although I'm only young, I know that gymnastics isn't sustainable. And I'm an ambitious person, I always want to keep achieving things, so I've had to be smart and think about the future.

I've always enjoyed wearing things that are different or unique.

One of the best things about fame, though, is the feedback I get from parents and kids. The fact there are so many kids wanting to get involved in gym and that their parents are happy to use me as someone for them to look up to is really flattering and it gives me reassurance that what I'm doing is still alright, that I'm still a role model. After all, I am a gymnast and I'm trying to lead by example.

But I don't let that stop me from having a life. Everyone has a laugh, goes out and has fun, and it's not like I come falling out of clubs drunk, being sick and having to be held up by the bouncer. I just go out and enjoy myself, like everyone else.

It's funny, because when you come out of a club and the photographers are waiting, they 'pap' you and the flashes are going off for about 10 seconds, but they'll always use the one picture where you're half blinking and it looks as though you're drunk. Yet there'll be another picture from the same night in a different paper and you'll look completely fine. It's one of the tricks of the paparazzi trade.

These days it's not only my hair that seems to attract attention, but my clothes too, especially if I'm out in Peterborough. In London, anything goes, but I do get funny looks with some of the outfits I wear at home. I definitely have a passion for clothes and fashion so it's something I'd love to get into a bit more one day. I've always enjoyed wearing things that are different or unique and I love the idea of taking an outfit that I can see in my head and turning it into something I can actually wear.

At the moment, I end up searching through the shops in desperation, looking for the things I've got in my head, which is frustrating. I think I'd like to have my own fashion label or clothing range. Not trying to be the next Vivienne Westwood or some kind of massive superstar – that wouldn't be me – but the world of fashion is something I'd definitely like to try my hand at.

A good suit, skinnies, nice ties and bow ties are all important, although I've got a lot more than that spilling out of my wardrobe. It's important to have a nice selection of shoes, too. I've probably got around fifty pairs, which gives me options for lots of different outfits. I'm not snobby about what I wear, so it doesn't have to be designer, it can come from any kind of high street brand. If it looks good, I'll wear it.

My end goal – the one that's always on my mind – is my future and the happiness of the people around me.

I had clothes and shoes filling an entire room – and bursting out of it – in my old house, which was one of the reasons I needed to move to a bigger place. I'd grown out of the little two-bed house that I moved into when I was with Billie, so I started having a bigger house built before the London Olympics. It's a three-bed chalet bungalow on some land that's not too far from where she lives, funnily enough.

It was tricky, because when I bought the land I didn't know how much money I would be earning, so I wasn't sure if by the time I was fitting it out, I'd be having to look for bargains or if I'd be able to splash out a bit more. But, as time went on, I found I could start pushing the boat out and get stuff like oak flooring, little lights going up the stairs and built-in speakers installed all around the house.

I've added a lot of personal touches, like the two stained glass windows either side of the fireplace in my living room that have etched into them the same angel wings that are tattooed on my back. The big fireplace was important to me because I wanted the house to be cosy. I didn't want it to be too contemporary with sharp edges or cold, steel surfaces, I wanted it to be warm with huge, soft sofas that you can sink right into. And it's pretty much perfect, for now.

Because I was away for most of the time when it was being built, Mum helped out with it a lot. She was amazing. She drove the costs down, employed the contractor and managed all the finances. Basically, she sorted out all the dull but really important bits. She'd always ring to run stuff by me first, but I would occasionally have to correct her when she said, 'Louis, I think we should have . . .' 'No Mum. It's *my* house, remember?'

I would love to be able to buy her a house one day, a retirement home so she doesn't have to do anything because she's worked so hard. I was able to buy her a car a few years ago but I want to do more. A huge part of my motivation when I'm competing or doing anything is that I want to do well for Mum. My end goal – the one that's always on my mind – is my future and the happiness of the people around me and I'd love to be able to give something back to my mum because she's always given so much to me.

But I did manage to forget to tell her one of my biggest ever bits of news last year. It was Gab who received the letter in early December – a very formal one addressed to Mr Louis Antoine Smith Esq. He opens all my stuff because otherwise it wouldn't get read until about four months later, and when he read that I was being made an MBE in the Queen's New Year Honours List he was buzzing.

He was bursting to tell everyone, but wanted to speak to me first. I was in the studio, spending the whole day rehearsing for the *Strictly*

Christmas special, so by the time we spoke it was about 10.30 p.m. I just remember saying to him, 'Are you sure?' I had to double-check because it was so nuts. I'm only a gymnast – in sports like that you just feel a bit out of the loop from the mainstream. And the fact that I didn't even win gold; it just goes to show that nothing is ever out of reach.

I was overwhelmed but Gab told me I couldn't tell anyone and when someone says that to me I normally just forget what they tell me, so that I don't get into trouble. It was only about three weeks later, when Gab asked me if I'd told my mum yet that I was like, *Oh, shit*.

It's such a great honour to be recognised and to know that even though I didn't win gold, the scale of the achievement has been understood. For me, it wasn't about silver or gold when the margins between them are so small, and the team medal too was such an historic moment for the sport in this country. The only thing that could have made me happier was for Paul to get the same recognition, so when I found out he was also getting an MBE, I was so happy.

When I was younger, Paul was away from his family a great deal, because I always wanted him to come to competitions with me, so he sacrificed a lot to help me get to where I am today. He deserves every award going for all he's done for me and my teammates, as well as for Huntingdon Gym and the whole sport during his career.

Receiving my MBE from the Queen was actually a bit of a reunion for us, because I met her after Beijing, too, when all the medallists were in one room and she went round us all – first the gold medallists, then all the silver medallists and then the bronze medallists. She came over to me and said, 'You're the gymnast.' When I said that yes, I was, she asked if I could do something right there and then. I don't know what I was thinking, but it was one of those times when you're nervous and stuff just comes out of your mouth. I said, 'Look, I know you're the Queen, but I'm suited and booted . . .' So I'm the guy who said 'no' to the Queen – which probably makes it even more surprising that she decided I was worthy of honouring with an MBE.

The award was the perfect way to end the most exhilarating, emotional roller coaster of a year I've ever experienced. And it closed a chapter that started way back when Mum first took me to that gym in Werrington to watch my brother learn the basics.

When the London Olympics were announced in 2005, I was still living at home and didn't have any responsibilities, so it became a goal for me. It came at an age when you start setting targets. Beijing was a stepping stone, but London 2012 was always *the* one.

When you have such a massive goal like that, you tend not to look beyond it. You don't plan for what comes next because all your energy is focused on that one thing. So when everyone started asking me about going on to compete at the Rio Olympics in 2016, I honestly had no idea whether I wanted that or not.

I went to Beijing and won bronze, and I stayed at the top for the next four years, which is hard to do in a sport like gymnastics. Then I rose to the immense pressure of 2012 and did the best routine I could possibly have done in front of a huge home crowd. So even if I were to qualify for Rio – and it would be very tough with the quality of young gymnasts coming through now – do I really want to train for more than 30 hours a week for the small chance of winning something that probably wouldn't better the feeling of winning a medal at my home Olympics? I'm not sure anything can live up to that. So I've made no plans for Rio. If I get back in the gym and the bug comes back then, maybe. But it's a maybe that gets fainter with every passing day.

Whether or not I go on to compete in Rio, I would like people to remember me as someone who did something no Brit has ever done before in the sport of gymnastics. And as someone who helped to get the sport back on track and put it in a new light, so that people start to become aware of it and follow it a bit more.

Growing the sport will take time – it's not something that can happen overnight – but things are at least better now than when I was younger. It was a huge challenge back then to get sponsors involved in the sport.

But people are a lot more interested in it now. The next step is to push for something bigger, for something that will really help to secure the future of gymnastics in Britain.

But that is for the future. For now, and for the first time since I can remember, I don't have a set target in my head and there's no plan written on a white board in the gym that I have to complete before the week is over. Gymnastics is a sport where you know what you're doing every single day for every week of the year. So for the first time in my life, I'm looking at a blank canvas, but it's one with plenty of opportunities bubbling beneath the surface. I'm looking forward to dipping in and finding out which one is the best fit for me and what the next chapter holds for Louis Smith.

e first time in my life, I'm looking at a blank canvas.

Whatever does come next though, I'll dive right into it. I don't really know any other way of doing things. I've spent the past 24 years of my life working hard, both in the gym and out of it, to become a better athlete and someone worthy of being called a role model.

It has been physically and emotionally painful at times but for me, there's no better feeling than achieving something you've dreamed about. So no matter how many mornings I woke up with my back in agony, ankles reluctant to move and arms still heavy with the efforts of the previous day, I never once thought 'I don't want to do this anymore'.

Instead, I used the drive and energy that made me such a nightmare as a kid to help me achieve something I never thought was possible when I was growing up on a Peterborough council estate. A lot of people thought I'd never get there, I never listened to them. A lot of people laughed at my ambition, I never listened to them, either. Now I've won three Olympic medals and proved that the five words which appeared in my head after I won my first World Championship medal, and that are now forever inscribed on my back, are true: What I Deserve I Earn.

This edition first published in Great Britain in 2013 by
Orion
an imprint of the Orion Publishing Group Ltd
Orion House, 5 Upper St Martin's Lane,
London WC2H 9EA
An Hachette UK Company

10 9 8 7 6 5 4 3 2 1

A CIP catalogue record for this book is available
from the British Library.

Hardback ISBN: 978 1 409 14556 1

Designed by carrdesignstudio.com
Printed in Great Britain by Butler, Tanner & Dennis

MIX
Paper from
responsible sources
FSC® C023561

www.orionbooks.co.uk

Picture Credits

AJP Media: page 38–39, Andy
Hooper, *Daily Mail*, Solo Syndication:
page 10–11, 120–121, 131 (bottom
left), 180–181; BBC: page 6, 196, 203,
206, 208–209, 214, 217, 221, 222;
Ben Duffy: page 107, 127; Digital
Sports / Steve Mitchell: page 65;
Getty Images: page 5, 16, 28–29, 48,
72–73, 75, 90, 93, 108, 123, 133, 145,
154, 157, 164, 170–171, 174, 184–185,
188–189,192, 194, 199, 235; John
Ord / www.johnordphotography.
com: page 102; Levon Bliss: page
20; Pal Hansen: page 26–27, 34–35,
68, 136–137, 160, 193, 224, 239; Mark
Oblow / www.markoblow.com: page
84–85; Rex Features: page 2–3, 36,
44–45, 52–53 (background only),
54–55, 58, 61, 70, 80–81, 82–83, 94,
98–99, 101, 112–113, 128–129, 134,
138–139, 141, 146–147, 151,167,
176, 190–191, 205, 210, 213, 229;
Simon Lipman (photography)
/ www.katyeellisagency.com,
Gareth Scourfield (styling), *Esquire*
magazine: page 88–89, 152–153